Mark A. Finley

W9-BGR-646

Revive
US AGAIN

Pacific Press® Publishing Association
Nampa, Idaho
Oshawa, Ontario, Canada
www.pacificpress.com

Cover design by Steve Lanto
Cover design resources from iStockphoto.com
Inside design by Aaron Troia

Scripture quotations are from The New King James Version, copyright
© 1979, 1980, 1982, Thomas Nelson, Inc., Publishers.

The author assumes full responsibility for the accuracy of all facts and
quotations as cited in this book.

You can obtain additional copies of this book by calling toll-free 1-800-
765-6955 or by visiting http://www.adventistbookcenter.com.

Library of Congress Cataloging-in-Publication Data:

Finley, Mark, 1945-
  Revive us again / Mark A. Finley.
    p. cm.
  ISBN 13: 978-0-8163-2450-7 (hard cover)
  ISBN 10: 0-8163-2450-6 (hard cover)
  1. Revivals. 2. Evangelistic work—Seventh-day Adventists. I. Title.
BV3790.F5415 2010
  269—dc22

                                                        2010039427

11 12 13 14 • 5 4 3 2

CONTENTS

A PERSONAL MESSAGE
FROM MARK FINLEY

As you begin your personal journey through the pages of *Revive Us Again,* let me assure you that you are poised on the verge of one of the most thrilling spiritual breakthroughs of your life. I am confident that the Holy Spirit will lead you to a closer walk with Jesus as you peruse these chapters.

My intent in writing this book is not to present some new, startling, sensational information on revival and the Holy Spirit. Although you will discover vital new truths as you read, my real goal is to lead you through God's Word and the writings of Ellen G. White to life-changing spiritual principles.

As you meditatively read each chapter, take time to prayerfully consider the practical implications of what you are reading. As you do, your mind will be open to the deep moving of the Holy Spirit. You will place yourself in an atmosphere of spiritual renewal.

These chapters are to be prayerfully experienced—not merely rapidly read to get through the material as quickly as possible. Each chapter concludes with an Application page. These Application pages are especially designed to lead you into a prayer and devotional experience for spiritual revival. You will also be led to practical faith-sharing experiences and witness opportunities.

Two powerful statements from the writings of Ellen G. White have guided me in the writing process. I have kept them foremost in my mind.

"A revival of true godliness among us is the greatest and most urgent of all our needs" (*Selected Messages,* bk. 1, p. 121).

"There is nothing that Satan fears so much as that the people of God shall clear the way by removing every hindrance, so that the Lord can pour out his Spirit upon a languishing church and an impenitent congregation. If Satan had his way, there would never be another awakening, great or small, to the end of time" (*Review and Herald,* March 22, 1887).

There is nothing that the Seventh-day Adventist Church needs more than a genuine spiritual revival. There is nothing that Satan fears more than this promised revival. There is nothing more important for church administrators, pastors, and church members than seeking this revival together. There is no greater priority.

What possibly could be more critical for the people of God than the outpouring of the Holy Spirit in Pentecostal power for the finishing of God's work on earth? This must be at the top of every board-meeting agenda on all levels of church structure. But revival always begins with one man, one woman, one boy, or one girl on his or her knees, seeking God. You can be that one person who is used of God to bring spiritual revival to your home, your church, your school, or your conference.

God's promise is for you. "If My people who are called by My name will humble themselves, and pray and seek My face, and turn from their wicked ways, then I will hear from heaven, and will forgive their sin and heal their land" (2 Chronicles 7:14). The Word of God is sure. His promises are certain.

Throughout history, God has sent revivals in response to the prayers of His people. In our day, the long awaited end-time revival will come. The Holy Spirit will be poured out. The work of God on earth will be finished. Jesus will return and we will soon go home.

As you read these pages, may the prayer of your heart be, "Lord, revive us again."

CHAPTER ONE

Prayer and Revival

The greatest revivals in the history of the world have been the result of earnest, heartfelt intercession. The sparks of revival are kindled on the altar of prayer. Revival and prayer are indissolubly linked. Without persevering, prevailing prayer, there is no corresponding power. Ellen White could not be clearer in stating this divine reality. "A revival need be expected only in answer to prayer" (*Selected Messages,* bk. 1, p. 121).

The New Testament church was bathed in prayer. The believers heeded Jesus' admonition to "wait" for the promise of the Father (Acts 1:4). They believed as they sought God together that they would receive "power" when the Holy Spirit descended from heaven upon them (Acts 1:8).

The Acts narrative is plain. Speaking of those early disciples, it states, "These all continued with one accord in prayer and supplication" (Acts 1:14). In response to these faith-filled prayers, the Holy Spirit was poured out powerfully on Pentecost. Three thousand were baptized in a day. And the record states, "They continued steadfastly in the apostles' doctrine and fellowship, in the breaking of bread, and in prayers" (Acts

2:42). These early Christians united in world-changing prayer. And their prayers made a difference. "When they had prayed, the place where they were assembled together was shaken" (Acts 4:31). "And with great power the apostles gave witness to the resurrection of the Lord Jesus" (Acts 4:33). The disciples gave themselves continually to prayer (Acts 6:4).

Through prayer, Peter was led to the home of Cornelius, a Gentile, and new vistas were open for the proclamation of the gospel (Acts 10:1–33). When the early church united in prayer, God sent an angel from heaven to deliver Peter from prison. Prayer was at the heart of the New Testament churches' power.

Prayer and the early Advent movement

Prayer was also at the very heart of the early Advent movement. The pioneers of the Advent movement were great men and women of prayer, sometimes spending a good portion of the night in prayer. Describing her experience in these prayer sessions, Ellen White writes, "At our important meetings, these men [early Advent leaders] would meet together and search for truth as for hidden treasure. I met with them, and we studied and prayed earnestly; for we felt we must learn God's truth. Often we remained together until late at night, and sometimes through the entire night, praying for light, and studying the word. As we fasted and prayed, great power came upon us" (*Manuscript Releases,* vol. 3, p. 413).

Ellen White constantly urged these early Adventists to seek God in prayer. "The greatest victories gained for the cause of God are not the result of labored argument, ample facilities, wide influence, or abundance of means; they are gained in the audience chamber with God, when with earnest, agonizing faith men lay hold upon the mighty arm of power" (*Gospel Workers,* p. 259).

Believing that the second coming of Christ was imminent, these early Adventists humbled their hearts, confessed their sins, and interceded for their families, friends, and communities.

In March of 1840, William Miller conducted a series of prophetic lectures in the Casco Christian Church in Portland, Maine. Hundreds crowded into the church. Some stayed from early morning until late at night. The Holy Spirit moved powerfully upon the congregation. In her book *Life Sketches,* Ellen White describes the impact of these meetings.

"Terrible conviction spread through the entire city. Prayer meetings were established, and there was a general awakening among the various denominations, for they all felt more or less the influence that proceeded from the teaching of the coming of Christ" (*Life Sketches,* p. 137). Speaking of this revival in Portland, Maine, F. D. Nichol adds, "Little prayer meetings have been set up in almost every part of the city" (*The Midnight Cry,* p. 29).

Here is a certainty regarding genuine revival. Prayer initiates revival. Prayer sustains revival. Prayer nurtures revival, and prayer follows revival.

Revivalist Leonard Ravenhill put it this way, "Without exception, all true revivals of the past began after years of agonizing, hell-robbing, earth-shaking, heaven-sent intercession. The secret to true revival in our own day is still the same.

But where, oh, where, are the intercessors?"

Welsh Revival

One of the greatest revivals in history was the Welsh Revival of 1904. Twenty-six-year-old Evan Roberts had been praying for thirteen years that his life would be totally controlled by the Holy Spirit. He pled with God for an undivided heart—a heart totally committed to the kingdom of God. Evan often prayed late into the night, interceding for the teens and the young adults in his church. He especially prayed regularly that God would visit Wales with revival power. The Welsh Revival began at a youth meeting in Evan Roberts's own church, Moriah Loughor, when he shared his own experience with God. Evan urged his friends to seek the infilling of God's Spirit in their own lives. The Holy Spirit touched hearts. Sixteen young people were converted. The sparks of revival begun in this humble village church would ignite the flames of revival throughout the country. It is estimated that within nine months, one hundred thousand people were converted in the tiny country of Wales. The crime rate dropped. Drunkards and prostitutes were transformed by God's grace. Pubs reported losses. Lloyd George, once prime minister of England, wrote that on one Saturday night at the height of the Welsh Revival one tavern sold only nine cents' worth of liquor. Many taverns were transformed into places of prayer.

Political meetings and soccer matches were delayed or even postponed because the churches were packed with praying people. Often these prayer services lasted six to eight hours at a time. Hardened, spiritually calloused Welsh coal miners crowded into these spirit-filled services and returned to the mines changed men. Profanity disappeared from their lips and never returned. It was reported that the pit ponies in the mines failed to understand the commands of these born-again miners who now, without cursing, seemed to speak the language of heaven.

The revival weakened around 1906, but its impact on tens of thousands of lives continued. When one elderly lady was asked why the Welsh Revival seemed to fade away, she quickly responded, "It has never been extinguished. It is still burning in my heart." It had burned in this godly woman's heart for more than seventy years.

An entire nation was changed because a young man, Evan Roberts, and a group of his young friends took our Lord's example of passionate intercession seriously.

A nation changed by prayer

Alfred Lord Tennyson was certainly correct when he said, "More things are wrought by prayer than this world dreams of." One of the most dramatic moments in recent memory is the fall of the Berlin Wall. Few realize the mighty, concentrated prayer movement that led up to the breathtaking events in East Berlin on November 9, 1989. In 1982, Christian Führer, a young German pastor in Leipzig, opened the doors of his church each Monday evening for prayer and discussions on freedom. These prayer sessions grew until one Monday night in October of 1989, eight thousand people crowded into the church. Thousands more stood outside the Nikolai Church. A nationwide freedom movement was birthed in the cradle of prayer. People by the tens of thousands in villages, towns, and cities across East Germany joined the Leipzig intercessors. On that Monday night in October, nearly one million people were praying for freedom. Twenty years after the fall of the Berlin Wall, commenting on the absolute necessity of earnest intercession, Pastor Christian Führer declared, "We realized that if we stopped praying, there would be no hope for change in Germany" ("Prayer and the Berlin Wall," *Cimarronsong* (blog), February 12, 2009, http://cimarronsong .wordpress.com/2009/02/12).

One former communist government official who had worked with the Stasi, or East German secret police, gave this amazing testimony. "We were ready for anything, except for candles and prayer." The Berlin Wall could not stand before the sound of the fervent prayers of God's people united in seeking Him.

Ellen White states a similar truth about the power of prayer. "At the sound of fervent prayer, Satan's whole host trembles" (*Testimonies for the Church,* vol. 1, p. 346). Prayer makes a difference. Intercessory prayer is powerful. Just as the Berlin Wall fell as God's people prayed, so the walls that keep us from an intimate experience with Jesus fall as we plead with God. The walls that hold back the mighty revival that God longs to send to His church crumble at the sound of earnest intercession. Walls of pride, prejudice, anger, bitterness, lust, complacency, lukewarmness, and materialism all give way to the moving of the Holy Spirit through prayer.

Prayer is an absolute necessity if revival is going to take place. A. T. Pierson makes this insightful observation: "From the Day of Pentecost, there has not been one spiritual awakening in any land that has not begun in a union of prayer. Though only among two or three; no such outward, upward movement has continued after such prayer meetings have declined" (quoted in Arthur Wallis, *In the Day of Thy Power*, p. 112).

In prayer we humble our hearts before God, acknowledging our total dependence upon Him. In prayer we unite with David pleading, "Create in me a clean heart, O God, and renew a steadfast spirit within me" (Psalm 51:10). We confess with Daniel, "We have not obeyed the voice of the LORD our God, to walk in His laws, which He set before us by His servants the prophets" (Daniel 9:10). We cry out with Paul, "O wretched man that I am! Who will deliver me from this body of death?" And with the apostle in prayer, our faith grasps the promises of God and we joyfully exclaim, "I thank God—through Jesus Christ our Lord!" (Romans 7:24, 25).

Prayer opens our lives to God's cleansing power. During prayer, the Holy Spirit X-rays our souls. We see hidden sins and defects in our characters that keep us from being the powerful witnesses He longs for us to be. Prayer draws us into an intimate relationship with Jesus. In prayer, we open our minds to the guidance of the Holy Spirit. We seek His wisdom, not our own.

Prayer and the great controversy

Prayer also enables God, in the context of the great controversy between good and evil, to work more powerfully than if we had not prayed. This conflict between Christ and Satan is a battle between the forces of hell and the forces of righteousness. The struggle is real. Thousands upon thousands of good and evil angels are involved. The Bible's last book, Revelation, describes the battle this way: "Michael and His angels fought against the dragon and his angels" (Revelation 12:7). One-third of the angels in heaven rebelled against God (Revelation 12:4). These forces of evil bring disappointment, disease, disaster, and death to our world. The forces of righteousness bring joy, peace, health, and life.

Each one of us also participates in this conflict. Ours is a planet in rebellion against God. When our first parents, Adam and Eve, yielded to the temptations of the evil one, they forfeited their God-given dominion of this planet. Satan became the "ruler of this world" (John 12:31). The Bible also calls him "the prince of the power of the air" (Ephesians 2:2). In this great controversy, "we do not wrestle against flesh and blood, but against principalities, against powers, against the rulers of the darkness of this age, against spiritual hosts of wickedness in the heavenly places" (Ephesians 6:12).

Prayer is the weapon to defeat the powers of hell. "The weapons of our warfare are not carnal but mighty in God for pulling down strongholds" (2 Corinthians 10:4). Through prayer we give God permission to move mightily in our behalf. In this universal struggle, God voluntarily limits Himself. He does not violate our power of choice. God will never force anyone to serve Him.

He is doing everything He can, within the ground rules of the conflict between good and evil, to save all humanity. Whether I pray or not, He is reaching out to my family members. Whether they pray for me or not, He is working in my life. Whether I pray or not, there is a measure of protection that God gives through angelic beings.

But when I pray and seek Him, I open up through prayer new channels that enable God, in the context of the conflict between good and evil, to do things that He would not do otherwise. God not only respects the power of choice of people who are not praying, He respects my power of choice as I pray. "It is a part of God's plan to grant us, in answer to the prayer of faith, that which He would not bestow did we not thus ask" (*The Great Controversy,* p. 525).

As we pray, God pours out His spirit through us. Prayer enables the illimitable God to help those in need. A marvelous passage in the Bible, 1 John 5:14–17, describes what happens when we pray. Many passages in the Bible encourage us to pray. But this passage does more than admonish us to pray. It does more than urge us to pray. It does more than encourage us; it actually explains why prayer is so effective. In 1 John, chapter 5, verses 14–16, the apostle declares, "Now this is the confidence that we have in Him." Our confidence is not in our prayers. Our confidence is not in our faith. Our confidence is in Him. The apostle continues, "If we ask anything according to His will, He hears us. And if we know that He hears us, whatever we ask, we know we have the petitions that we asked of Him." We can have absolute confidence that as we come to God, He will hear our petitions.

The next verse reveals what happens when we intercede for someone else. "If anyone sees his brother sinning a sin which does not lead to death." The sin which leads to death is the unpardonable sin. It is the point at which people have hardened their hearts against God. "He will ask." Who is the *he* who is doing the asking? It is the intercessor. What happens? "He [God] will give him [the intercessor] life for those who commit sin not leading to death." God pours out His life through us to touch the life of someone else. We are the channels through which God pours out His illimitable power. God honors our heartfelt intercession for someone else. It is intercessory prayer that makes a difference.

The prayer life of Jesus

Jesus is our great model in intercession. He regularly retreated to a quiet place to pray. He sought God for strength to meet the challenges of the day. He pleaded with His Father for strength to overcome Satan's temptations. The Gospel of Mark records one of Jesus' early morning prayer sessions in these words: "Now in the morning, having risen a long while before daylight, He went out and departed to a solitary place; and there He prayed" (Mark 1:35). If Jesus, the Divine Son of God, understood that prayer is a necessity, don't we need prayer much more in our own lives? Jesus recognized that inner spiritual strength comes through prayer. Luke's Gospel records Jesus' prayer habits. "He Himself often withdrew into the wilderness and prayed" (Luke 5:16). Prayer was not something Jesus did occasionally when a need or problem arose. Prayer was a vital part of Jesus' life. It was the key to staying connected to the Father. It was the essence of vibrant spirituality. Jesus' prayer life was a vital part of His life. Daily the Savior renewed His relationship with His Father through prayer. Jesus' prayer life gave Him courage and strength to face temptation. He came from these prayer sessions with a spiritual freshness and deepened commitment to do the Father's will. Describing one of these prayer times, Luke adds, "As He [Jesus] prayed, the appearance of His face was altered, and His robe became white and glistening" (Luke 9:29). Jesus radiated the strength that comes from moments in God's presence through prayer. If Jesus, the Divine Son of God, needed time in His Father's presence to overcome the fierce temptations of Satan, we certainly need time in God's presence much more.

Jesus was never too busy to pray. His schedule was never too packed to spend time with His Father in communion. He never had so much to do that He rushed in and out of His Father's presence. Jesus came from these intimate times with God spiritually revived. He was filled with power because He took time to pray.

R. A. Torrey laments the busyness of today's Christianity, which at times is so powerless. Torrey says, "We are too busy to pray, and so we are too busy to have power. We have a great deal of activity, but we accomplish little; many services but few conversions; much machinery but few results."

Ellen White makes the same point. "Many, even in their seasons of devotion, fail of receiving the blessing of real communion with God. They are in too great haste. With hurried steps they press through the circle of Christ's loving presence, pausing perhaps a moment within the sacred precincts, but not waiting for counsel. They have no time to remain with the divine Teacher. With their burdens they return to their work" (*Education*, p. 260).

One thing is for certain. We cannot face the devil in our own strength. Prayer is the answer. Through prayer God bathes us with His presence and power. Through prayer He touches the hearts of our loved ones. Armored with prayer, we can face the enemy at the end times. It is impossible to live godly lives in the end times with an inconsistent prayer life. When our connection with God is broken, our power from God is cut off. When there is little prayer, there is little power. Prayer is our humble acknowledgment that we cannot live the Christian life without His strength. It is the admission of our inability to cope with Satan's temptations alone. Through prayer we are more than able to handle Satan's temptations. The devil is no match for the praying, trusting child of God.

On our knees, pleading with God, we will experience miracles. We will see God's hand move in miraculous ways. As Jesus did, we will come from these seasons of prayer refreshed and invigorated. We will sense that God is working through our prayers to transform the lives of others around us as well.

Would you like to experience a spiritual revival in your own life? Do you desire a renewed spiritual experience? Are you tired of spiritual complacency? Do you long for a spiritual revival in your church?

Our Lord has promised to answer the earnest longings of His children. He will respond as we seek Him. His promises are ours. He has said, "If My people who are called by My name will humble themselves, and pray and seek My face, and turn from their wicked ways, then I will hear from heaven, and will forgive their sin and heal their land" (2 Chronicles 7:14).

Jesus adds this promise: "If you then, being evil, know how to give good gifts to your children, how much more will your heavenly Father give the Holy Spirit to those who ask Him!" (Luke 11:13).

Four life-changing prayer principles

If you will incorporate the four basic prayer principles outlined below as a regular part of your devotional life, God will pour out His Spirit on you abundantly. Your spiritual life will be revived, and God will use you as a catalyst for revival in your home, your school, your workplace, your neighborhood, and your local church.

1. Set aside a specific time each day to be alone with God.

Place top priority on this uninterrupted quiet time alone in God's presence. Many have found the ACTS model helpful as a guide to keep their minds focused during their devotional times. You, too, may find it helpful in keeping your thoughts from wandering in your prayer times.

A—Adoration
C—Confession
T—Thanksgiving
S—Supplication

A—Adoration

Begin your prayer time with a period of adoration and praise. Praise God for who He is and what He means to you. The psalmist declares that God inhabits the praises of His people (Psalm 22:3). Another psalm states, "Whoever offers praise glorifies Me" (Psalm 50:23). Praise lifts our minds from who we are to who He is. It directs our attention to His greatness not our weakness, to His wisdom not our ignorance, and to His might not our feebleness.

C—Confession

Ask God to humble your heart and reveal anything in your life not in harmony with His will. Openly confess the attitudes, habits, and practices He convicts you of that are not Christlike. Confession clears the way for the Holy Spirit to work mightily in our lives. We are told that the disciples entered into this kind of deep soul searching just before Pentecost. "These days of preparation were days of deep heart searching. The disciples felt their spiritual need and cried to the Lord for the holy unction that was to fit them for the work of soul saving" (*The Acts of the Apostles,* p. 37). The Holy Spirit was poured out on these seeking disciples who humbled their hearts in repentance and confession.

T—Thanksgiving

Think of very specific things God has done for you recently and thank Him. The apostle Paul instructs us to "be filled with the Spirit, speaking to one another in psalms and hymns and spiritual songs, singing and making melody in your heart to the Lord, giving thanks always for all things to God the Father in the name of Jesus

Christ" (Ephesians 5:18–20). List the things you are thankful for. Do not take God's blessings for granted. Thank Him for what He has done for you. You may not be a gifted singer, but let Him place a song of gratitude in your heart during your prayer times and break forth in songs of thanksgiving to the One who is so good to you.

S—Supplication

God is absolutely delighted when we come as little children dependent on our heavenly Father with our requests. Jesus assures us to "Ask, and it shall be given to you" (Matthew 7:7). James admonishes us to "ask in faith without doubting." (James 1:6). Paul was confident that "my God shall supply all your need" (Philippians 4:19).

We can kneel before the throne of God with the absolute assurance that we will "obtain mercy and find grace to help in time of need" (Hebrews 4:16). Bring to Him the desires of your heart. Ask Him to make your heart one with His so your desires are His desires.

The more time we spend with God, the more time we will long to spend in His presence. The Christian life is about knowing God. The more we know Him, the more we will love Him. The ACTS model of prayer will help us to know Him even better.

Our second principle of a revitalized devotional life is this:

2. Read the Bible prayerfully, allowing the Holy Spirit to impress your mind.

Let God's Word become the subject matter for your prayers.

If prayer is the breath of revival, Bible study is its heart. Prayer and Bible study are the Siamese twins of revival. They are interconnected. The more your pray, the more you will hunger for God's Word. The more you study the Word, the more you desire to pray. Here are a few practical suggestions.

   a. Take one psalm at a time. Read a few verses. Ask what God is saying to you in these verses. Speak to Him in prayer about what the Holy Spirit impresses you. As you pray through the Psalms, you will hear God's voice speaking to your own heart as He spoke to the psalmists.

   b. You may also want to concentrate your devotional life on the last scenes of Christ's life. The Bible contains six chapters on the death of Christ—Psalm 22, Isaiah 53, Matthew 27, Mark 15, Luke 23, and John 19. Take one chapter at a time. Read a few verses. Visualize the sufferings of Christ for you. Let the Holy Spirit impress you with His enormous sacrifice. You will find your heart broken over your sins that led Him to the cross. You will be strangely warmed by His love, drawn to Him by His grace, and overwhelmed by His sacrifice.

Study the great passages of the Bible prayerfully. It will make a significant difference in your devotional life. Let God speak to you through His Word. Pray with the psalmist, "Revive me according to Your word" (Psalm 119:154).

If we follow this counsel of God's last day messenger, we

will see marvelous results. "Take the Bible, and on your knees plead with God to enlighten your mind. If we would study the Bible diligently and prayerfully every day, we should every day see some beautiful truth in a new, clear, and forcible light" (*Review and Herald,* March 4, 1884).

We now come to our third principle of a revived prayer life.

3. Learn to pray aloud.

Secret prayer is not necessarily silent prayer. Often during our daily activities, it is appropriate to send up silent petitions. During our devotional times, praying aloud keeps the mind concentrated on God. Jesus prayed aloud.

The disciples were so impressed when they heard the Savior praying aloud that they asked Him to teach them to pray like He did (Luke 11:1). In Gethsemane, Jesus committed Himself to do the Father's will at any cost. Matthew's Gospel records that Jesus fell on His face three times saying, "Not My will but Thy will be done." Obviously, Jesus was praying out loud (see Matthew 26:36–44).

The book of Hebrews tells us that Jesus "offered up prayers and supplications, with vehement cries and tears to Him who was able to save Him from death" (Hebrews 5:7).

Again Ellen White instructs us to "learn to pray aloud where only God can hear you" (*Our High Calling,* p. 130). We need not fear that somehow Satan is listening to our prayers, knows what we are praying, and is preparing some strategy to deceive us for we are assured that "at the sound of fervent prayer, Satan's whole host trembles" and God answers our petitions by sending legions of angels, causing

Satan's host to fall back (*Testimonies,* vol. 1, p. 346).

Follow the example of Jesus by praying aloud during your devotional time. At first it may be a little difficult, but as you continue, the Holy Spirit will lead you into a rich experience with the Master.

This leads us to our fourth principle of prevailing prayer and spiritual revival.

4. Organize a small prayer group of three to five people and covenant to meet together at least once a week to pray.

The New Testament church united in praying for the power of the Holy Spirit (Acts 1:14; 4:31). Jesus instructed His disciples to pray together. "Again I say to you that if two of you agree on earth concerning anything that they ask, it will be done for them by My Father in heaven. For where two or three are gathered in My name, I am there in the midst of them" (Matthew 18:19, 20).

Commenting on this passage, Ellen White adds, "The promise is made on the condition that the united prayers of God's people are offered, and in answer to these prayers there may be expected a greater power than that which comes in answer to private prayer. The power given will be proportionate to the unity of the members and their love for God and for one another" (*The Central Advance,* February 25, 1903). This is an amazing statement full of encouragement for God's people today. There is special, unusual power in praying together. When we put aside our personal agendas, unite in prayer, and pour out our hearts to God, He answers far beyond our expectations.

The history of revival is the rich history of a praying people. It is the history of the church seeking God together. The church is revived when members establish multiple prayer bands and pour their hearts out to God.

Why not begin a prayer band in your home? Why not invite a few friends to join you in seeking God for a deeper spiritual experience? Why not intercede with a few close companions for your family, friends, and neighbors who may not know Jesus and His message for our time?

A praying father or mother can make an incredible difference in the lives of their children. A praying husband or wife can make an amazing difference in their marriage. Praying church members can make a huge difference in their church. Prayer groups make a difference in the community. Praying students can change the atmosphere in their school. The legacy of prayer giants such as Moses, Joseph, and Daniel demonstrates that praying people change the course of history.

Do you want to plant the seeds of revival? Bathe your life in prayer. Cover your family with prayer. Saturate your neighborhood with prayer. Intercede for your spouse, your work associates, your friends, and your neighbors. Lift up your petitions to the God who hears. Seek the One whose ear is always bent low, listening for the requests of His children. Open your heart to a Savior who is more interested in answering your prayers than you are in praying.

When you do, you will have discovered the all-essential key to revival for both your own life and God's end-time church.

My Personal Application

"Revival signifies a renewal of spiritual life, a quickening of the powers of mind and heart, a resurrection from the spiritual death" (*Review and Herald*, February 25, 1902). Revival occurs not simply as we read about it, but as we put into practice the biblical elements of revival. The New Testament church maintained a vital experience with Jesus through prayer, Bible study, and witnessing.

This is the first of a series of practical applications of the spiritual principles we will discuss in each chapter. As you put these principles into practice in your own life, you will discover the key to personal spiritual revival. Your experience with Jesus will be deeper and more intimate than you ever thought possible.

Each application section will focus especially on the theme of the chapter that you have just read. Listed below is a devotional exercise for this coming week. You can use it as an outline for your prayer life.

In chapter 1, we have introduced the ACTS model of prayer. As you kneel before God:

1. Choose three specific things to praise Him for. Spend a few moments simply adoring Him.
2. Think of something specific in your life that is not in harmony with His will and confess that one thing to Him.

3. Choose three things to thank Him for.
   a. Regarding some personal trait in your own life
   b. Regarding your family
   c. Regarding your church family

Present the greatest need in your life right now before God and claim the promise in Philippians 4:19, "My God shall supply all your need according to His riches in glory by Christ Jesus."

CHAPTER TWO

The Holy Spirit and Revival

I had just completed a seminar on revival in a local church, when an old man approached me. Evidently, he had been a Christian for many years. Politely this elderly gentleman inquired if he could ask me a question. When I responded positively, he quickly began referring to various Bible passages. It was obvious he knew the Bible quite well. At first I wondered where he was going with his comments, but then he came to the heart of his question.

Is the Holy Spirit a divine influence, a force emanating from God, or is the Holy Spirit the Third Person of the Godhead? Many Christians are confused on this point.

Is the Holy Spirit a power flowing from God as some sort of impersonal influence, or is the Holy Spirit a divine person? I explained to my new friend that this question is of enormous importance.

If the Holy Spirit is the Third Person of the Godhead equal with the Father and Son but we think of Him as an impersonal influence, we are robbing a divine person of the honor, respect, and love which is His alone. If the Holy Spirit is a mere influence or power, we will try to grasp this power and use it. But if we recognize the Holy Spirit as a person, we will yield to His influence, surrender to His guidance, open our hearts to His instruction, and yield to His will. Our only desire will be to allow Him to use us.

A genuine spiritual revival is the work of the Holy Spirit. We cannot revive ourselves. Only the Holy Spirit can bring revival. Writing with prophetic insight, Ellen White states it this way: "A revival of true godliness among us is the greatest and most urgent of all our needs. We must have the holy unction from God, the baptism of his Spirit; for this is the only efficient agent in the promulgation of sacred truth. It is the Spirit of God that quickens the lifeless faculties of the soul to appreciate heavenly things, and attracts the affections toward God and the truth" (*Gospel Workers*, 1892 ed., p. 370).

It is absolutely vital to understand who the Holy Spirit is and how He works if we are to experience true revival. The false concept of the Holy Spirit as merely a power or force can lead to self-exaltation. "Look at the power I have." In contrast, the true concept of the Holy Spirit as the Third Person of the Godhead leads to surrender to His will.

Unfortunately, many Christians in churches around the world do not have a clear understanding of who the Holy Spirit is or His work in their lives. Dr. Bill Bright, the founder and former president of Campus Crusade for Christ, points out that his organization has surveyed "thousands of Christians in churches around the world" and sadly, "nearly 95 percent of the respondents have indicated that they have little knowledge of who the Holy Spirit is or why He exists."

A. W. Tozer writes, "The idea of the Spirit held by the

average church member is so vague as to be nearly nonexistent." Jesus' teaching on the Holy Spirit in the Gospels is crystal clear. Yet for the average Christian, according to Tozer, it is "vague" or "nearly nonexistent."

What a tragedy. Understanding the Bible's teaching on the Holy Spirit is absolutely vital for a growing Christian life.

In his book *The Secret: How to Live with Purpose and Power,* Dr. Bright shares his deepest convictions about Christian living in these words: "I am personally convinced that if today's Christians better understood the Bible's basic teaching about the Holy Spirit and then invited Him to release His power in their lives each day, they would experience unprecedented joy and personal fulfillment. More than that, our verbal and nonverbal witness for Jesus Christ would sweep the world" (p. 34).

Would you like to experience unprecedented intimacy with God? Would you like to receive Christ's supernatural power to live a victorious Christian life? Would you like to be a powerful witness for Jesus in the world? Understanding who the Holy Spirit is and receiving Him into your life is the key to a fulfilled Christian life.

Who is the Holy Spirit?

It is quite easy for us to think of the Father as a person and Jesus as a person. Our minds form mental images of Them. But the Holy Spirit is considered so mysterious and is so invisible, so secret, and His presence so universal that at times we question who He is.

Here is the mistake we make. We often equate divine personality with visibility. If the Holy Spirit is universal and present everywhere, we conclude the Spirit must be the force or presence of God but not a divine being. There are two major problems with this kind of thinking.

First, it is a human attempt to explain divine reality. It is attempting to shape divine truth to our limited way of thinking. It tries to break down the sublime truth of the Godhead into bite-size pieces so we can digest it. At times we forget that God is God!

We will never understand the complexity of all of His ways. As one eminent theologian said, "To try to understand the Trinity is to lose one's mind. To deny the Trinity is to lose one's soul."

The good news is that we do not have to understand everything about something to appreciate the something we may know only partially. I don't understand everything about electricity, but I am not going to sit around in the dark until I understand it.

Similarly, although we may not fully grasp everything about the nature of the Holy Spirit, we can receive the biblical teaching on the Spirit by faith and invite the Divine Guest to take up residence in our hearts.

There is another serious problem with the idea that the Holy Spirit is merely a force or the powerful influence of God and not the Third Person of the Godhead.

Second, the idea is contrary to the Holy Scriptures. The Bible contains three plain New Testament passages describing the Divine Trio in the Godhead. None of these passages makes One of the Godhead inferior or of lesser value than any Other. Our Lord's last command to His disciples was, "Go therefore and make disciples of all the nations, baptizing them in the name of the Father and of the Son and of the Holy Spirit" (Matthew 28:19). When New Testament believers became Christians, they entered into a divine fellowship, a heavenly oneness with the Father, Son, and Holy Spirit.

In Ephesians 2:18, the apostle Paul describes the unity of purpose in the Godhead in these words: "Through Him [Christ] we both have access by one Spirit unto the Father"; and the apostle describes the unity of the Godhead in Hebrews 10:9–15 with these descriptions: the Father wills, the Son works, and the Spirit witnesses.

Throughout Scripture the Father, Son, and Holy Spirit cooperate to accomplish Heaven's purposes in the plan of redemption. They are present at Creation, at Jesus' baptism, throughout Jesus' life, at the Cross, at Christ's resurrection, and during His ministry in the heavenly sanctuary.

The apostle Paul concludes his second letter to the Corinthians with these insightful words: "The grace of the Lord Jesus Christ, and the love of God, and the communion of the Holy Spirit be with you all. Amen" (2 Corinthians 13:14).

This passage speaks of three things: God's love, Christ's grace, and the Holy Spirit's communion.

In the Old Testament, God revealed His love through the warnings and instructions of the Old Testament prophets. In the New Testament, God revealed His love through the life and death of Jesus. We call this grace. Since the resurrection of Jesus and the inauguration of His ministry in the heavenly sanctuary, God reveals His love through the personal presence or communion of the Holy Spirit in our lives.

It is through the Holy Spirit we are brought into fellowship with the Father and the Son. It is through the Holy Spirit we enter into intimate communion with the Divine. Before Christ came in the flesh, the Father was the most conspicuous Person of the Godhead, filling the horizon; when Jesus came, He filled the horizon. The New Testament world saw God's love through Jesus. This is why Jesus said, "He who has seen Me has seen the Father" (John 14:9).

Once Jesus ascended to heaven, we entered into a new dispensation. The dispensation of the Holy Spirit! The Holy Spirit is just as real, just as much a Divine Person, just as much a Member of the Godhead as the Father and the Son. The Holy Spirit is not a thin, shadowy influence emanating from the Father. He is not an impersonal force, something to be vaguely recognized, or just an invisible principle of life.

The Holy Spirit is a Divine Person!

LeRoy E. Froom in his book *The Coming of the Comforter* puts it this way: "Jesus was the most marked and influential personality ever in this old world, and the Holy Spirit was to supply His vacated place. No one but a person could take the place of that wondrous person. No mere influence would ever suffice" (p. 41).

Ellen White offers this clarification: "There are three living persons of the heavenly trio; in the name of these three great powers—the Father, the Son, and the Holy Spirit—those who receive Christ by living faith are baptized, and these powers will co-operate with the obedient subjects of heaven in their efforts to live the new life in Christ" (*Evangelism,* p. 615).

Like a trio making heavenly music with each singing different parts, the Father, Son, and Holy Spirit harmoniously unite Their voices in a song of salvation to redeem us. The Holy Spirit is indeed the Third Person of the Godhead. Listen to these powerful words: "Evil had been accumulating for centuries and could only be restrained and resisted by the mighty power of the Holy Spirit, the Third Person of the Godhead, who would come with no modified energy, but in the fullness of divine power" (*Testimonies to Ministers,* p. 392).

The Holy Spirit came with the fullness of divine power on the early disciples at Pentecost. It is Heaven's plan that the Holy Spirit comes with the fullness of divine power on every believer.

In John 14–16, Jesus describes the ministry of the Holy Spirit in detail. These are probably some of His most significant words. His teaching on the Holy Spirit is life transforming.

The importance of this tremendous truth regarding the Holy Spirit cannot be overemphasized. Here are Jesus' own words: "I will pray the Father, and He will give you another Helper, that He may abide with you forever, even the Spirit of truth, whom the world cannot receive, because it neither sees Him nor knows Him: but you know Him, for He dwells with you and will be in you" (John 14:16, 17).

Through the ages past, the Holy Spirit had been with faithful believers; but from Pentecost forward, God's purpose was that He "will be in you." This is a divine reality. These are not just nice religious words. The world believes what it sees. We live in a world where seeing is believing. Twenty-first century men and women often rule out the supernatural. If you cannot touch it, if it is not material, if you cannot quantify it, then it does not exist.

For the secular person to think of the Holy Spirit dwelling in the life of the believer is ridiculous. It is preposterous beyond belief. But this is precisely Christ's point. What the world does not understand and certainly cannot comprehend, Christians grasp by faith.

The First and Second Persons of the Godhead, the Father and the Son, take up residence in our hearts through the Third Member of the Godhead, the Holy Spirit.

We are no longer orphans. We are not like an abandoned child. We have not been left on the street corner of this world by a Christ who has ascended to some heavenly mansion and left us alone. From time to time, we read about a baby abandoned, left at the door of a city apartment wrapped in a few light blankets and discovered by the neighbors. Revealing His personal presence through the Holy Spirit, Jesus reassures us, "I will not leave you orphans; I will come to you" (John 14:18).

Our loneliness ceases. Inside, we have no gnawing emptiness, longing for companionship and love. Jesus fills us with His personal presence through the Holy Spirit. At times we hunger for the personal presence of Christ. Through the Holy Spirit, we have Jesus abiding in our souls.

Commenting on John 14:16–18, Ellen White speaks of the descent of the Holy Spirit on the disciples.

Pentecost brought them the presence of the Comforter, of whom Christ had said, He "shall be in you." And He had further said, "It is expedient for you that I go away: for if I go not away, the Comforter will not come unto you; but if I depart, I will send Him unto you." . . . Henceforth through the Spirit, Christ was to abide continually in the hearts of His children. Their union with Him was closer than when He was personally with them (*Steps to Christ,* pp. 74, 75).

Think of it. It is really incredible. Today our union with Jesus through the Holy Spirit can be closer than if we had been one of His disciples two thousand years ago. We can have a more intimate relationship with Jesus today through His Holy Spirit than His followers had before Pentecost.

Ellen White puts it this way. "The work of the Holy Spirit is immeasurably great. It is from this source that power and efficiency come to the worker for God; and the Holy Spirit is the comforter, as the personal presence of Christ to the soul" (*Review and Herald,* November 29, 1892).

What is this work of the Holy Spirit which is so immeasurably great in the life of Christ's followers? What does this precious heavenly gift desire to do for each follower of Christ? What is Jesus longing to do through the gift of the Holy Spirit in your life?

The Holy Spirit is our personal Helper

In John 14:16, Jesus declared, "I will pray the Father, and He will give you another Helper, that He may abide with you forever." In John 16:7, the Master adds, "If I do not go away, the Helper will not come to you; but if I depart, I will send Him to you."

Twenty-four times in John, chapters 14, 15, and 16, the personal pronouns of *He, Him,* and *whom* are applied to the Holy Spirit. He is our personal Helper.

The New Testament was written in Greek. The Greek word translated "helper" is the word *paraclete.* This is a wonderful word. It literally means "called to the side for the purpose of helping." Some translations use the word *advocate.* An advocate was a legal assistant in the Roman court system called to one's aid in a court of justice.

According to Leon Morris in his commentary on John's Gospel, "Any friend who would take action to give help in a time of legal need might be called a 'paraclete' or 'advocate' " (p. 665). The *paraclete* is one who stands with us at all times comforting, instructing, strengthening, guiding, and filling the future with hope.

Have you ever been around someone who, though struck by tragedy and heartache, seems to radiate a supernatural peace in the midst of their tears? Most likely the Holy Spirit, the Friend who comforts and encourages all believers, dwells in their hearts. God's Spirit does not shelter us from human hurts. Jesus Himself experienced the full gamut of human pain and emotional trauma. He felt isolated and alone as He bore the guilt of our sins on the cross.

But in the midst of our pain, we have One who stands by our side—a Friend who gives us peace that passes all human understanding. The Holy Spirit is our personal Comforter, who can give us supernatural strength, courage, and peace when all around us things seem to be crumbling.

One night just after I had given one of my prophecy lectures in Los Angeles, I received word that one of our staff was feeling quite ill and had fainted. Along with others, I hurried into the auditorium to check on his status. It soon became obvious that he was experiencing the symptoms of a heart attack. We immediately called 911 and rushed him to the hospital. Although things appeared to go well for the first couple of days, his condition suddenly worsened. Before the physicians could operate, this staff member died. What amazed me then and continues to amaze me today is the peace the Holy Spirit gave to his wife in the midst of this heartbreaking, unexpected tragedy. Through her sorrow and in the midst of her pain, she had an inner peace. The Holy Spirit was there helping, comforting, encouraging, and guiding her as a friend.

The King James Version translates John 14:16 as Jesus sending "another Comforter." In Latin, the word for *comfort* comes from two words, *com* meaning "with" and *fortes* meaning "strengthen."

The Holy Spirit dwelling in our hearts is like a close friend whom we can trust to give us strength to face whatever the evil one throws at us today.

Help for our daily needs

What weaknesses are part of your genetic makeup? What temptations have you yielded to again and again? What sins seem to continually trip you up? Is it anger, lust, or bitterness? Is it some physical addiction out of control, or is it possibly a critical spirit? God is fully aware of the spiritual battle that wages in each person's soul. He has sent His Holy Spirit as our Helper to overcome the powers of darkness that enslave us. He has sent the Holy Spirit to sever the chains that bind us and to set us free.

He has sent the Holy Spirit so we can face the enemy with strength. Revival takes place when we open our heats to the powerful ministry of the Holy Spirit in our lives. "None are so vile, none have fallen so low, as to be beyond the working of this [Holy Spirit's] power. In all who will submit themselves to the Holy Spirit a new principle of life is to be implanted; the lost image of God is to be restored in humanity" (*Christ's Object Lessons,* p. 96).

Through the power of the Holy Spirit, an entire change can be made in your life.

The Holy Spirit is our personal Teacher

In John 14:17, Jesus speaks of the Holy Spirit as the "Spirit of truth." In John 16:13, Jesus declares, "When He, the Spirit of truth, has come, He will guide you into all truth; for He will not speak on His own authority, but whatever He hears He will speak; and He will tell you things to come."

The Holy Spirit is our personal Teacher to instruct us in the ways of eternity as we read God's Word. There is no truth we need to know into which the Holy Spirit is unprepared to guide us.

The only way we can understand God's Word is through the Holy Spirit. Some people study God's Word to prove others wrong. Others study God's Word seeking divine truth through human wisdom. They bring all the faculties of the mind to try to understand the Bible, but they are still confused.

The book *Steps to Christ* describes our need to have the Holy Spirit help us understand the Bible. "We can attain to an understanding of God's word only through the illumination of that Spirit by which the word was given" (p. 114). The same Holy Spirit that inspired the prophets to write the Bible inspires us as we read it today. Our Divine Teacher reveals the deep and hidden things of God's Word as well as our own hearts.

In the recesses of our hearts lurk hidden sins, attitudes, and thought processes that are contrary to the principles of Christ. The Holy Spirit brings these secrets into the light of day so we can deal with them. The Holy Spirit constantly teaches as we study God's Word to lay our doubts, fears, anxieties, and worries at Jesus' feet.

The same Holy Spirit who revealed truth to the Bible prophets as they wrote the Bible, reveals truth to us as we study it. The psalmist prayed, "I am afflicted very much; revive me, O LORD, according to Your word" (Psalm 119:107). He continues his petition, "Plead my cause and redeem me; revive me according to Your word" (Psalm 119:154). The Word of God is the foundation for all revival. The Holy Spirit leads us to apply God's Word personally.

Consider saying this prayer: "Jesus, I realize I cannot understand Your Word without Your Spirit. As I read Your Word, I give the Holy Spirit permission to convict me of sin, instruct me in righteousness, and impress me of the urgency of living in the judgment hour. Oh, Lord, whatever truth You have for me, I desire it. Whatever changes You want in my life, I want them. Oh, divine heavenly Dove, come and instruct me."

The true Vicar of Christ on earth does not sit on a papal throne in Rome. The true Vicar of Christ on earth is the Holy Spirit, sent from the throne room of the universe as our Teacher and Instructor into all truth.

There is yet another aspect of the Holy Spirit's ministry we must not overlook.

The Holy Spirit is our personal Guide in the decision-making processes of life

As your personal Guide, the Holy Spirit will convict you of unconfessed sin. He will seek to prevent you from falling in the first place by convicting of wrong before you do it. He may bring a scriptural command to your mind. He may give you a sense of definite conviction about something you are going to do. The Holy Spirit will steer you toward God's will in all the decisions of life.

John 16:13 describes the Holy Spirit as the One who guides us. In Isaiah 58:11, God promises, I "will guide you continually." Psalm 32:8 adds, "I will instruct you and teach you in the way you should go; I will guide you with My eye."

1. God guides us through the inner convictions of the Holy Spirit.
2. He guides us through the Spirit-inspired passages in His Word.
3. He also guides us as the Holy Spirit impresses others to share words of wisdom and counsel.

4. Sometimes God guides us by allowing the Holy Spirit to so arrange providential experiences in our lives that a plain path opens before us, and we sense which way God is leading us.

However God is leading us, it is through His Holy Spirit.

The dove man

Many years ago, there was a guide in the desert of Arabia who never got lost. He carried in his robes a homing pigeon with a long fine cord attached to its leg. When in doubt as to the path to take, he tossed the pigeon into the air, and the pigeon quickly strained at the cord as it tried to fly in the direction of home. People called that guide the "dove man."

The Holy Spirit, the heavenly Dove, will lead us home. Open your heart to Him. Come before God honestly with this prayer: "Lord, I surrender my will to Yours. I surrender my selfish ambitions to You. Lord, whatever You want me to do, I will do it.

"Whatever habits You desire me to give up, I will surrender them. Lord, You are my Helper, my Teacher, my Guide. I long for You to dwell in me through Your Holy Spirit, today and always."

The Holy Spirit will bring revival into our lives. "The baptism of the Holy Ghost as on the day of Pentecost will lead to a revival of true religion and to the performance of many wonderful works" (*Selected Messages*, bk. 2, p. 57).

Now is the time to seek for the baptism of the Holy Spirit

and genuine revival. Will you open your heart to the heavenly Dove today?

Holy Spirit, light divine,
Shine upon this heart of mine.
Chase the shades of night away,
Turn my darkness into day.

My Personal Application

In this chapter, we have discussed the ministry of the Holy Spirit in the life of each Christian. One of the works of the Holy Spirit is to place in each of our hearts the desire to see others saved in God's kingdom. Just as the Holy Spirit guided Philip to the Ethiopian, Peter to Cornelius, and Paul to the jailer at Philippi, so God leads us to men and women today to share His love.

This week in your devotional life, pray earnestly for specific people. Moses pled for God's people. Daniel interceded for Israel. Jesus prayed for Peter by name (Luke 22:31, 32). Paul prayed for Christians in Ephesus, Philippi, and Colossae. The more specific we are in our prayers, lifting up our families, friends, neighbors, and work associates, the more powerfully God will work. With your Bible open, claim the following promises.

Matthew 7:7—"Ask, and it will be given to you; seek, and you will find; knock, and it will be opened to you."

1 John 5:14—"Now this is the confidence that we have in Him, that if we ask anything according to His will, He hears us."

Hebrews 4:16—"Let us therefore come boldly to the throne of grace, that we may obtain mercy and find grace to help in time of need."

As you claim these promises, write the names of three people on the lines below and pray for them daily.

1._____

2._____

3. _____

The Urgency of Revival

The story is told of a woman who frantically phoned her insurance agent. The conversation went something like this:

> **Woman:** Mr. Johnson, I need to increase the insurance on my house immediately.
>
> **Insurance agent:** Madam, I would be delighted to increase your coverage. You will need to come to my office to fill out and sign the appropriate paperwork.
>
> **Woman:** I would like to do it now over the phone.
>
> **Insurance agent:** That is not possible. You will have to come by the office, or I will be happy to come out to your home later in the week.
>
> **Woman:** Sir, you do not understand. I want to increase my coverage today.
>
> **Insurance agent:** I wish I could help you, but there are a few documents you must sign.
>
> **Woman:** Look, mister, my house is on fire; I have to increase my coverage now!

There are some things in life that you just cannot put off until tomorrow. They have to be done today, or the consequences may be catastrophic. Some things matter little if we put them off until tomorrow, but other things we put off to our eternal loss.

Preparation for the second coming of Christ is one of those absolutely vital things that cannot be delayed. The second coming of Christ may seem to be delayed, but our preparation for His return should never be delayed.

In Matthew 24, Jesus discusses the signs of His return. In Matthew 25, the Savior discusses preparation for His return. Matthew, chapter 24, focuses on what's going on in the world before Jesus returns. Matthew, chapter 25, focuses upon what's going on in the church before Jesus returns.

After discussing false christs and prophets, wars, pestilences, earthquakes, natural disasters of all types, rising crime and violence, and a host of other signs just before His return, the Savior warned, "Watch therefore, for you do not know what hour your Lord is coming. . . . Therefore you also be ready, for the Son of Man is coming at an hour you do not expect" (Matthew 24:42–44).

In Matthew 25, Jesus gives us the first of three parables about what it means to "watch" and "be ready" for His coming. The parable of the ten virgins speaks with special relevance to the church today. Mathew's Gospel lists twenty-one of Jesus' parables. Of those twenty-one parables, fourteen refer to the kingdom of God or the church.

In these parables, Jesus is especially concerned about the spiritual condition of His people. These kingdom-of-God parables do not focus on the world; they focus on the church.

Commenting on the significance of the parable of the ten virgins, Ellen White says, "I am often referred to the parable of the ten virgins, five of whom were wise, and five foolish. This parable has been and will be fulfilled to the very letter" (*Review and Herald,* August 19, 1890).

This parable is so important, so significant, so vital for the church today that God brought it to the prophet's mind repeatedly.

The parable begins with these words: "The kingdom of heaven shall be likened to ten virgins who took their lamps and went out to meet the bridegroom" (Matthew 25:1).

While each kingdom-of-heaven parable refers to the church, the story of the ten virgins speaks especially to the church waiting for the return of our Lord.

In the Bible, a woman represents the church, the bride of Christ. Virgins represent the pure, true church, undefiled with corrupt doctrines. The number ten is used because ten is the smallest number of Jewish men that could comprise a synagogue. This story is obviously speaking about God's true church at the end time. The lamps represent the Word of God. The psalmist David writes, "Your word is a lamp to my feet and a light unto my path" (Psalm 119:105).

The members of this Bible-believing church with pure doctrine have the light of God's Word to illuminate the world with His truth as they wait for the Bridegroom's return.

"Now five of them were wise, and five were foolish" (Matthew 25:2).

Notice that the story does *not* contrast the righteous and

unrighteous virgins, the holy and the unholy virgins, or the good and bad virgins. Neither does it contrast the obedient and disobedient virgins, the loyal and rebellious virgins, or the faithful and the unfaithful virgins. Instead, the Bible calls them the "wise" and "foolish" virgins.

We may logically ask the question, What made one group "wise," and what made the other group "foolish"? Was one group wise because they were awake, and another group foolish because they were asleep? Evidently not! Matthew 25:5 states, "While the bridegroom was delayed, they all slumbered and slept." The wise as well as the foolish were sleeping. The startling reality of this parable is not that five virgins are sleeping but that they all are.

Living on the knife edge of eternity, on the verge of the kingdom of God, the entire church is pictured as spiritually drowsy, asleep to the great opportunities to prepare the world for the coming of the Bridegroom. The secular, materialistic, godless culture around us lulls us into spiritual stupor.

God's people are a people with a message, a people with a mission, a people raised up to powerfully share the light of His Word with a world in darkness.

Isaiah foretells the destiny of the church in these words,

"Arise shine;
> For your light has come!
> And the glory of the LORD is risen upon you.
> For behold, the darkness shall cover the earth,
> And deep darkness the people;
> But the LORD will arise over you,

And His glory will be seen upon you.
The Gentiles shall come to your light,
And kings to the brightness of your rising.
"Lift up your eyes all around, and see:
They all gather together, they come to you"
    (Isaiah 60:1–4).

Empowered by the Holy Spirit, filled with the oil of His grace, God's people will illuminate the world with His glory. They will impact the world with His truth. The gospel will be preached to the ends of the earth. The mission will be accomplished. The task will be completed. The work will be finished. The way will be prepared for the Bridegroom's return. The path will be lighted with the torch of truth.

This is our destiny. This is our calling. This is the reason for our existence as the people of God. There is no other reason for the existence of the Seventh-day Adventist Church.

But the foolish virgins fail to participate in this closing work of God on earth. They miss this magnificent opportunity. And they miss out on eternity. Why? They are all members of the true church. They are all waiting for the coming of the Bridegroom. They all anticipate our Lord's return. They all accept and believe the truths of Scripture. They all are doctrinally orthodox. They all live morally upright lives. They all enjoy the fellowship of the church and the companionship of the wise virgins.

Let's study the lives of these foolish virgins a little more closely. Let's look at what Inspiration says about them. "Those who were foolish took their lamps and took no oil with them" (Matthew 25:3).

In the ancient world, lamps could hold only a limited supply of oil. Wise people always took a small flask of extra oil. When the oil in the lamp was exhausted, they were able to replenish the supply. Notice carefully, it is not that the foolish virgins had no oil. It is they did not have enough.

"While the bridegroom was delayed, they all slumbered and slept.

"And at midnight a cry was heard: 'Behold, the bridegroom is coming; go out to meet him!' Then all those virgins arose and trimmed their lamps. And the foolish said to the wise, 'Give us some of your oil, for our lamps are going out.' But the wise answered, saying, 'No, lest there should not be enough for us and you; but go rather to those who sell, and buy for yourselves.' And while they went to buy, the bridegroom came, and those who were ready went in with him to the wedding; and the door was shut.

"Afterward the other virgins came also, saying, 'Lord, Lord, open to us!' But he answered and said, 'Assuredly, I say to you, I do not know you.'

"Watch therefore, for you know neither the day nor the hour in which the Son of Man is coming" (Matthew 25:5–13).

A casual reading of this parable brings to light this obvious fact: the foolish virgins lacked the all-essential oil. The oil, of course, represents the Holy Spirit. Yet there are many symbols of the Holy Spirit in the Bible. Fire, water, and wind are just a few. Why does Jesus use the symbolism of oil here? There are at least three reasons.

Throughout the Old Testament, oil symbolized total, complete consecration. It represented a setting apart for holy use. The sanctuary and all of its articles, as well as the priests, were consecrated with oil.

Oil represented healing. The good Samaritan anointed the wounded traveler with oil. James 5 speaks of anointing the sick with oil. In a sense, the oil represents the healing power of the Holy Spirit to heal our hearts from the scars of sin.

Oil also symbolized illumination or witnessing. The lamps of the sanctuary were lighted with the golden oil.

God longs to have a people filled with His Spirit, totally consecrated to Him. He longs to heal them of bitterness, envy, and jealousy. He longs to deliver them from pride, arrogance, self-inflated importance, gossip, lust, and impurity. He longs for them to witness of His grace and hold their lighted torches of witness high to fulfill their destiny in illuminating the way for the coming of the Bridegroom.

The foolish virgins depended on oil they had acquired in the past. The foolish virgins made a spiritually devastating, fatal mistake. They had some oil but not enough. Unfortunately, they thought the limited supply of oil they had was sufficient.

But when the cry came, "Behold, the bridegroom is coming; go out to meet him!" they cried out, "Our lamps are going out" (Matthew 25:6). Their supply of oil was not sufficient for the unanticipated delay. Is it possible to assume that a superficial experience with God will get us through the great crisis that is coming? Have we forgotten the words of the prophet that we will "need an experience much higher, deeper, broader, than many have yet thought of having" (*Gospel Workers*, p. 274)?

The foolish virgins were part of the superficial, conservative class. Are you depending on a religious experience you had once upon a time but has long since slipped away? Are you depending on an experience with God that is in the past tense, not the present? Does your heart still burn within you as you open God's Word? Do you still sense His presence when you get on your knees to pray? Do you still love to take those long walks alone and pour out your soul to Him?

The foolish virgins trusted in their past experience as if they had all that was needed for their spiritual lives. The height of Christian folly is neglecting personal soul culture and believing everything is all right. The foolish virgins neglected to nourish their souls.

Ellen White puts it this way:

The class represented by the foolish virgins are not hypocrites. They have a regard for the truth, they have advocated the truth, they are attracted to those who believe the truth; but they have not yielded themselves to the Holy Spirit's working. They have not fallen upon the Rock, Christ Jesus, and permitted their old nature to be broken up. . . . The Spirit works upon man's heart, according to his desire and consent implanting in him a new nature; but the class represented by the foolish virgins have been content with a superficial work. They do not know God. They have not studied His character; they have not held communion with Him; therefore they do not know how to trust, how to look and live. Their service to God degenerates into a form (*Christ's Object Lessons*, p. 411).

The foolish virgins are content with a stale, superficial experience from the past, and although they acknowledge the truth, the truth has not transformed their lives. They still operate on the level of the old nature. The old nature dominates their thoughts and their actions. They know the theory of truth but have not been radically changed by it. They have a casual understanding of the doctrines of the church but not a heart experience with God. They have the outer without the inner. They have the form without the substance. They have the theory without the reality.

Ezekiel describes the foolish virgins' experience. "They come to you as people do, they sit before you as My people, and they hear your words, but they do not do them; for with their mouth they show much love, but their hearts pursue their own gain" (Ezekiel 33:31).

The apostle Paul points out that this will be the identifying characteristic of the unprepared who live just before Christ's second coming. He says, "In the last days perilous times shall come: For men will be lovers of themselves . . . lovers of pleasures rather than lovers of God, having a form of godliness, but denying its power" (2 Timothy 3:1–5).

From the outward appearance, everything looked fine. They had lamps in their hands. What more did they need?

They thought they were ready for the coming of the bridegroom. But there is a difference between having the Word in your hand to defend the truth and having the Word in your heart to live the truth. The foolish virgins were informed but not transformed. They were instructed in the Word but not changed by the Word. They were convicted of the truth but not changed through the truth. Doctrinal correctness does not save. Here is the essential question to ask ourselves: Has the truth that we believe, and the Christ we proclaim to others radically transformed our own lives?

God's last-day messenger explained what the foolish virgins lacked. "In the parable of the ten virgins, five of them are described as wise, and five as foolish. The foolish virgins took no oil in their vessels with their lamps. They did not obtain the grace of Christ. They were just like the wise virgins as far as theory and appearances were concerned. They had their lamps, but they had no oil. They made a profession, but they did not know what genuine conversion meant" (*Signs of the Times,* February 17, 1890).

Ellen White continues by describing the difference between mere belief and biblical faith.

Genuine faith works by love, and purifies the soul. There is a faith that has power to cleanse the life from sin. The devils believe that Christ came into this world as man's Redeemer, that he wrought mighty miracles, that he was one with the Father, that he died a shameful death to save fallen man. The devils believe that he rose from the dead, that he ascended into the heavens, and sitteth on the right hand of the Father. The devils believe that he is coming again, and that shortly, with power and great glory, taking vengeance on them that know not God and obey not the gospel. They believe all that is recorded in the Old and New Testaments. But will this faith save the demons of darkness? They have not the faith that works by love and purifies the soul. That faith, and that alone, which cleanses the soul-temple, is the genuine faith (*Signs of the Times*, February 17, 1890).

The foolish virgins hoped to make up for their lack by their association with the wise virgins. They hoped to get from them what they did not have for themselves. "The foolish said to the wise, 'Give us some of your oil, for our lamps are going out'" (Matthew 25:8).

The oil represents the sanctifying grace of the Holy Spirit that transforms the character and enables us to be lights of the world to prepare the way for the coming of the Bridegroom.

Here is the incredible good news. There is an abundant supply of heaven's oil for each one of us. There is no shortage of the power of the Holy Spirit to give us the victories we long for in our personal lives and the powerful witness we long to be to the world. But no one can be spiritual for us. Nobody else's prayers can substitute for our own. No one can study God's Word to receive His blessing for us. No one can have any intimate relationship with God for us. Someone else's prayer and Bible study will not transform our characters.

In the Bridegroom's absence, we have a tendency to slumber. It is easy to become complacent. The longer the delay, the greater the danger!

Jesus' words in Matthew 25:5—"While the bridegroom was delayed, they all slumbered and slept"—bring up another fundamental question that must be answered.

Why is the second coming of Christ delayed?

We are a people who should not be here. Jesus longed to come long ago. Why hasn't He come? Is He waiting for more famines, earthquakes, and wars? Certainly not! Let's examine three reasons why Christ has delayed His return.

Reason 1—Christ waits in love, suffering over the pain, agony, sorrow, poverty, sickness, and death of our world, waiting for the gospel to be preached with all power so all humanity will have an opportunity to be saved.

Both Matthew and Peter state this truth. "This gospel of the kingdom will be preached in all the world as a witness to all nations, and then the end will come" (Matthew 24:14). "The Lord is not slack concerning His promise, as some count slackness, but is longsuffering toward us, not willing that any should perish but that all should come to repentance" (2 Peter 3:9).

Ellen White points out the church's role. "By giving the gospel to the world it is in our power to hasten our Lord's return. We are not only to look for but to hasten the coming of the day of God. . . . Had the church of Christ done her appointed work as the Lord ordained, the whole world would before this have been warned, and the Lord Jesus would have come to our earth in power and great glory"

(*The Desire of Ages,* pp. 633, 634).

"He has put it in our power, through co-operation with Him, to bring this scene of misery to an end" (*Education,* p. 264).

Reason 2—Christ waits for His church to reveal His incredible character of love to a waiting world and watching universe. The Cross is the answer to the great controversy. Jesus' death on the cross answers Satan's charges. Our Lord now longs that a community of grace, His body, His church, reveal that His way brings life's greatest happiness. One of the basic New Testament principles relating to the second coming of Christ is the principle of the ripening harvest.

Jesus shares this harvest principle in Mark 4:28, 29: "The earth yields crops by itself: first the blade, then the head, after that the full grain in the head. But when the grain ripens, immediately he puts in the sickle, because the harvest has come." The principle of the ripening harvest suggests that Jesus will come when the seeds of righteousness are fully developed in the lives of His church and the seeds of wickedness are fully developed in the lives of those who reject His grace.

Ellen White affirms the harvest principle in this classic statement: "Christ is waiting with longing desire for the manifestation of Himself in His church. When the character of Christ shall be perfectly reproduced in His people, then He will come to claim them as His own" (*Christ's Object Lessons,* p. 69).

A waiting world and watching universe must see, once and for all, that the work of the Cross is finished in the lives of God's people.

In other words, God longs to develop a group of people at the end time who are passionate about knowing Him, absolutely convinced that His way is best, and consumed with sharing His love with others. They have been justified by His grace, sanctified through His grace, and are ready to be glorified because of His grace. Jesus is their Savior, their resurrected Lord, their living High Priest, and their long-awaited King.

Reason 3—Christ waits for the full manifestation of wickedness to be revealed in this world. Christ waits not only for a complete demonstration of His love to be revealed through His people but also for the seeds of rebellion to be fully mature in the hearts of those who reject His love. He must let wickedness, evil, and sin run its course so the whole universe will see the ultimate results of Satan's rebellion and will be secure in His love forever.

The book of Revelation describes two harvests. (1) The harvest of golden grain is a community of believers who reveal His grace and love through their obedience. (2) The harvest of grapes reveals the full display of rebellion, wickedness, and sin in our world. The two harvests reveal that God's way of redeeming love brings life and that Satan's way of selfishness brings death. "As the days of Noah were, so also will the coming of the Son of Man be" (Matthew 24:37).

Ellen White explains how wickedness must also mature. "God keeps a reckoning with the nations. . . . When the time fully comes that iniquity shall have reached the stated boundary of God's mercy, His forbearance will cease. When the accumulated figures in heaven's record books shall mark the sum of transgression complete, wrath will come" (*Testimonies*, vol. 5, p. 524).

"There is a limit beyond which the judgments of Jehovah can no longer be delayed" (*Prophets and Kings*, p. 417).

The church can hasten the coming of Jesus but it cannot delay it indefinitely. There will be a convergence of a praying, converted, transformed people revealing His glory, filled with His Spirit, proclaiming the message of His love and truth in a world of ever-increasing wickedness. God will one day soon declare before the universe, "It is finished; it is done. My people have revealed My character of love to a sin-polluted world. Every honest person on planet Earth has had a reasonable opportunity to respond to My grace and accept My truth, and Satan has demonstrated the depths of selfishness."

Our greatest danger—the danger of delay

The greatest danger that the foolish virgins faced was the danger of putting off a decision of enormous consequences. Spiritual complacency paralyzed them. Spiritual pride paralyzed them. They were blinded by self-congratulation. They were bathed in self-confidence. They were satisfied with what they had.

The foolish virgins never dreamed they were unprepared for the coming of the bridegroom. They failed to understand their lack. They were waiting for the coming of the bridegroom when they should have been preparing for the coming of the bridegroom.

The story is told of a strategy session Satan held with his evil angels. They were discussing how to keep human beings out of heaven.

One angel spoke up and said, "I will tell them there is no God."

Satan responded, "That will never work. The evidence from nature, the Bible, prophecy, and changed lives is too great. You must think of something else."

A second angel spoke up. "I will tell them there is no truth."

Satan responded, "You may deceive some that way, but thinking people recognize that just as there is scientific truth, there must be religious or moral truth. Think of something else."

A third evil angel came up with a brilliant idea. "I will tell them that there is no hurry. They have all the time in the world to prepare for the return of their Lord."

Satan agreed. "Tell them there is plenty of time. Tell them there is no need for urgency. Tell them to put off personal preparation. Tell them to wait until a more convenient time to deal with their inner attitudes. Tell them there is no need to be in any hurry at all about a personal relationship with God."

The story is fictitious, but its lesson is all too accurate.

Have you heard the whispers of the evil one in your ears? I have.

Is God calling you to do something that you are putting off? Is the oil in your lamp running low? Are you depending on an experience with God that you used to have? Are attitudes of jealousy, pride, or animosity toward others lurking deeply within your own heart? Do you become easily irritated with others and hold grudges? Do you overstate your accomplishments and exaggerate your successes to make yourself appear superior to others? God is calling for people in this last generation who know Him deeply, who love Him supremely, and who share Him passionately.

Would you like to commit yourself to being one of those people? The only way to be ready for the second coming of Christ is to get ready today and stay ready tomorrow.

Would you like to say, "Lord, knowing You is the most important thing in my life. If there is anything lurking in me that I may not be fully aware of, please reveal it to me. I am willing to surrender any habit or attitude not in harmony with Your will?"

If that is your desire, will you open your heart to Jesus right now? If possible, fall on your knees and ask Him to forgive your complacency. Plead with Him for a revival of true godliness in your own soul. Why not seek Him right now?

My Personal Application

Jesus said, "If two of you agree on earth concerning anything that they ask, it will be done for them by My Father in heaven" (Matthew 18:19). Ellen White adds, "Why do not two or three meet together and plead with God for the salvation of some special one, and then for still another?" (*Testimonies,* vol. 7, p. 21).

In a letter to Brother and Sister Farnsworth in 1903, commenting on Matthew 28:19, 20, the prophet of God pointed out that there can be greater power in the unified prayers of God's people than there is in private prayer (*Manuscript Releases,* vol. 9, p. 303). This week ask two other people to pray with you. Establish a prayer band and begin to meet weekly with your prayer partners.

Invite your prayer partners to join you in conversational prayer. In conversational prayer, each person prays in short sentences. After one person has prayed on one topic, another person prays, the second person confirms the prayer of the one who has prayed and adds a word of praise, thanksgiving, or request. In conversational prayer, each person prays multiple times aloud. The prayers of one person encourage another. God promises to answer powerfully from heaven as we seek Him together. He appoints the highest angels in heaven to answer our prayers. On the lines that follow, write the names of your prayer partners. Pray for and with them. Note the time of your weekly prayer appointment.

My prayer partners are:

1. _____

2. _____

3. _____

Our scheduled prayer time is:_____

CHAPTER FOUR

True and False Revivals

It was a violent land, in a violent time, and they were violent men. It was an immoral land, in an immoral time, and they were immoral men. It was a pleasure-seeking land, in a pleasure-seeking time, and they were pleasure-seeking men. Violence, lust, and pleasure-seeking walked hand-in-hand throughout the land.

The rich oppressed the poor, and the poor battled one another over meager resources. Nothing seemed to really satisfy. Their hearts were empty. Their souls were barren. Abandoning all restraints, they lived only for the moment. They lived by no standard except their own. Their restless, guilt-ridden hearts plunged them only further into pleasure-seeking.

Deep down inside, in the inner recesses of their hearts, where it really matters, they were empty. They were restless and needed peace. They were guilty and needed forgiveness. Their hearts were spiritually hungry, and they needed to be satisfied. Their wills were weakened, and they needed strength. They were confused and needed direction.

Then he appeared. A bearded, straight-talking, no-nonsense prophet clothed in camel's hair, preaching in some remote place by a river called the Jordan. He was not part of the religious establishment. He did not teach at one of Palestine's popular rabbinical schools. He had no titles or degrees. He did not hold any prominent position. He certainly was not some nationally known popular religious leader.

But this one thing he had—power. Whenever he spoke, lives were changed. They came by the thousands to hear his call for repentance, cleansing, and a new life. This man ripped aside all pretense and sham in religion and spoke directly to their hearts.

They called him John, John the Baptist. His message penetrated deep. His message hit home. His message convicted their conscience. His message transformed their lives. Compelled by the Spirit, they entered the Jordan and were baptized.

He spoke in the first century, but his message speaks to us again in the twenty-first century. He spoke at the beginning of the Christian era, but his message speaks at the end of time. He spoke to prepare men and women for the first advent of our Lord, but his message speaks to prepare men and women for the Second Advent, the return of our Lord.

John the Baptist's prophetic words regarding Jesus speak to our hearts today. "I indeed baptize you with water unto repentance, but He who is coming after me is mightier than I, whose sandals I am not worthy to carry. He will baptize you with the Holy Spirit and fire" (Matthew 3:11).

Notice this important passage carefully. John does not say, "He will baptize you with the Holy Spirit *or* fire." He says, "He will baptize you with the Holy Spirit *and* fire."

What is the significance of this phrase? Bible scholar Le-Roy E. Froom explains it this way: "It is an explanatory phrase, completing the idea. It is the scriptural way of repetition to emphasize and enforce a single thought. We are to be baptized with divine fire now to save us from destruction by consuming fire later" (*The Coming of the Comforter,* p. 268).

Throughout the Bible, fire is a symbol of the splendid glory, presence, and power of God. Fire is first mentioned in the Bible in Genesis, when an angel with a flaming sword guards the gates of Eden (Genesis 3:24).

It is obvious that this glorious being with the fiery sword represents the presence and power of God. Do you recall Moses' experience while tending sheep one night in the desert of Midian? He was amazed as he stumbled upon a burning bush—on fire but not consumed.

Moses records the story: "The Angel of the LORD appeared to him in a flame of fire from the midst of a bush. So he looked, and behold, the bush burned with fire, but the bush was not consumed. Then Moses said, 'I will now turn aside and see this great sight, why the bush does not burn.' So when the LORD saw that he turned aside to look, God called to him from the midst of the bush and said, 'Moses, Moses!' And he said, 'Here I am' " (Exodus 3:2–4).

The burning bush symbolized the fiery presence of God. When the Israelites built the sanctuary in the Old Testament, God's glory filled the Most Holy Place. His fiery presence dwelt between the golden cherubim on the ark of the covenant.

When Moses met God on Mount Sinai, the book of Exodus

records, "The sight of the glory of the LORD was like a consuming fire" (Exodus 24:17).

Israel was guided by a pillar of fire—the very presence of God—by night. From the fiery sword at the gates of Eden to Abraham's lamps of fire to Moses' burning bush at Horeb, fire represents the glorious presence of God. From the fire that enshrouded Sinai at the giving of the law to the flaming Shekinah glory that filled the Most Holy of Israel's sanctuary to the pillar of fire that guided Israel by night, fire represents the presence of God.

Consider the fire that fell on Elijah's altar as the man of God challenged the prophets of Baal or the fiery coal from heaven's altar that touched Isaiah's lips or the fire of Ezekiel's imagery—fire always is associated with God's presence and glory.

In the New Testament, fire represents the glorious presence of God through the Spirit. Fire and the Spirit are linked together on the Day of Pentecost. The Holy Spirit, symbolized by tongues of fire, filled the disciples. What, then, is the baptism of fire John speaks about? Baptism means immersion. Because fire is a symbol of the glorious presence of God, the baptism of fire is immersion in His presence.

This is a call for genuine, authentic Christianity. This is no call for something superficial. This is not a call for the outer without the inner. This is a call to allow the Holy Spirit to burn away all of the earthliness, rebellion, and lack of commitment in our lives and give us the warm glow of a genuine experience with God.

Commenting on this baptism with fire, Ellen White makes this powerful observation:

In all who submit to His power the Spirit of God will consume sin. But if men cling to sin, they become identified with it. Then the glory of God, which destroys sin, must destroy them. . . . At the second advent of Christ the wicked will be consumed "with the Spirit of His mouth," and destroyed "with the brightness of His coming.". . . The light of the glory of God, which imparts life to the righteous, will slay the wicked (*The Desire of Ages,* pp. 107, 108).

The personal presence of Christ through the Holy Spirit is a purifying presence. The Holy Spirit searches our inmost souls. The Holy Spirit penetrates our thoughts. The Holy Spirit cleanses our hearts and energizes our spiritual lives.

We have a choice whether to allow the purifying fire, the baptism of the Holy Spirit, to consume dross in our lives or to reject it and be consumed when "He will burn up the chaff with unquenchable fire" (Matthew 3:12).

The prophet Malachi puts it this way: "He is like a refiner's fire and like fuller's soap [soap for the outside, fire for within]. He will sit as a refiner and a purifier of silver; He will purify the sons of Levi, and purge them as gold and silver, that they may offer to the LORD an offer of righteousness" (Malachi 3:2, 3).

The Spirit is like a refiner's fire. Our God longs to consume sin in our lives. Through His Spirit, He will reveal our pride, selfishness, ambition, greed, critical attitudes, lustful thoughts, and bondage to destructive habits. If we allow Him to, the Holy Spirit will reveal aspects of our nature we have been blinded to previously.

Malachi the prophet declares that the Spirit sits to purify. He is not in a hurry. He is not impatient. He knows just how much to bring up the heat to purify our lives. If we are willing, He will continue until the process is complete.

Jesus is the "author and finisher" of our faith (Hebrew 12:2). The apostle Paul promises that we can be "confident of this very thing, that He who has begun a good work in you will complete it until the day of Jesus Christ" (Philippians 1:6). Jesus promises to work through the ministry of the Holy Spirit in our lives to complete what He has started. Do you know that Jesus has begun something in your life? Are you confident that He has started something in you? If you let Him, He will finish what He started. You may not be everything you want to be, but you are not what you once were. And the Holy Spirit is now appealing for you to go deeper.

Are you seeking a deeper experience in the things of God? Would you like the warmth of His presence to fill your life? Do you long to live a transformed life? Do you want God to use you in powerful ways to bless others?

God can never do something through us until He does something to us. God can never do something with us until He does something for us. God will never give us the gifts of the Spirit in their fullest measure unless we receive His cleansing and manifest the fruits of the Spirit.

Many Christians love to talk about the gifts of the Spirit. They talk about tongues, miracles, and prophecy. They want the outer when they have never experienced the inner. But God is not going to turn on Heaven's power if the electrical line is frayed.

Let me be very plain so you will not miss the point. If you long for miracles of healing but are not interested in God working a miracle in your life to deliver you from addictive habits, you are praying for the wrong miracle.

If you long to speak in tongues but have a critical tongue, you are praying for the wrong miracle. If you long to prophesy about the future, but are in bondage in the present, you are praying for the wrong miracle.

The power that God longs to give us today is the power to overcome our besetting sins. It is the power over addictive habits and lustful thoughts. It is the power over pride and self-inflated ego. It is the power over unkind words and thoughtless actions.

God wants to fill us up with kindness. He wants to fill us up with gentleness, meekness, self-control, love, joy, peace, faithfulness, and goodness (Galatians 5:22). This is the result of genuine revival. The result of the infilling of the Spirit is the manifestation of the fruits of the Spirit in our lives.

Life in the Spirit is full. It is full of God's presence. Percy G. Parker captures this baptism of fire in his poem "Burn in Me."

> Burn in me, fire of God
> Burn till my heart is pure;
> Burn till I love God fervently,
> Burn till my faith is sure.
>
> Burn in me, fire of God
> Burn deeper, deeper still;

Burn till my one and sole desire
Shall be the Father's will.

Burn in me, fire of God
Yea burn and burn again;
Till all I am by God consumed,
A "flame of fire" remain (quoted in Froom, p. 206).

This is the genuine baptism of the Holy Spirit. It is immersion in God's fiery presence so our hearts are one with Him. It is an infilling of His love so we have what He loves.

Old Dalmatia houses

Years ago in Old Dalmatia, the houses were made of bituminous limestone. This particular type of limestone is soft and easily cut and shaped. The entire house was made of it—walls, roof, floor—inside and out. But when it was finished it was uninhabitable, for it would reek with the strong odor of bitumen. The structure was completed by setting it on fire. It burned and burned, like coal, the fire sucking out the bitumen from the pores of the saturated stone, until everything combustible passed away in gas and smoke and the fire flickered and died out for lack of fuel.

Then the house was ready for occupancy; it stood, having the appearance of white marble, severely clean and habitable. And if later it was in the midst of a great fire, it would not burn, for there was nothing combustible left to burn. It was fireproof.

We, too, are by nature and through our wrong choices combustible, saturated with sin. The fires of the Holy Spirit can cleanse us now from sin's dominion so we can be delivered from sin's presence when Jesus comes. Our God is a "consuming fire" to sin wherever it is found (Hebrews 12:29). In the coming fires of God's final judgment, all elements of sin will be consumed.

Christ invites us to be baptized with the fire of His presence now to consume sin so we can avoid being consumed with sin later. This baptism of fire is a deep work of the Holy Spirit in our lives. It occurs as we give God time. It takes time for God to speak to us about anything in our lives not in harmony with His will. It takes time for Him to reveal those traits of character, those sinful habits and attitudes that keep us from really knowing Him. A deep spiritual experience with God cannot be rushed. This is why He urges, "Be still, and know that I am God" (Psalm 46:10).

The baptism of the Holy Spirit comes to us when we are on our knees praying with David, "Create in me a clean heart, O God, and renew a steadfast spirit within me. . . . Do not take Your Holy Spirit from me. Restore to me the joy of Your salvation, and uphold me with Your generous Spirit" (Psalm 51:10–12).

The Holy Spirit comes to us when we are quietly meditating upon His Word, seeking to live a more Christlike, godly life. There is a world of difference between the fire of God's presence that purifies us within and transforms our characters and the strange fire of the devil's kindling.

The true, genuine spirit of revival kindled by the Holy Spirit originates with God. It is from above. The false revival originates with the evil one and is from beneath. The true baptism of the Holy Spirit is based in God's Word and leads to victory over any trait of character or attitude that separates us from Jesus. The counterfeit manifestation of the Spirit is based in emotion and is more interested in signs, wonders, and miracles than in receiving a new heart. It exalts the gifts of the Spirit above the fruits of the Spirit.

It is more concerned with external power than with heart conversion.

The truth purifies and sanctifies. The false creates a religious excitement and sense of euphoria for the moment. At the end time as God pours out His Spirit among His people, Satan will attempt to counterfeit the work of God. He will attempt to deceive and mislead God's people.

The book of Leviticus tells the fascinating yet tragic story of Nadab and Abihu, the sons of Aaron. "Then Nadab and Abihu, the sons of Aaron, each took his censer and put fire in it, put incense on it, and offered profane fire before the LORD, which He had not commanded them" (Leviticus 10:1).

This certainly was not the fire of the Holy Spirit. It was false fire. These were the sparks of their own kindling. Nadab and Abihu substituted a counterfeit religious experience for the genuine. God did not accept this religious counterfeit, and "fire went out from the LORD and devoured them" (Leviticus 10:2).

God never accepts counterfeits. A counterfeit can deceive because it is so close to the genuine. You will never see a counterfeit three-, eleven-, or seventeen-dollar bill. Why not? There is no genuine. No counterfeiter in the world is foolish enough to counterfeit something that does not exist. The closer the counterfeit is to the original, the more likely the deception.

Satan's concern in the last days is not the unsaved world. He already has them in his grasp. His concern is Christians. By bringing his deceptions into the church, he will mislead millions. Our Lord has not left us without warning. He has given us clear light on the road ahead. "We also have the prophetic word made more sure, which you do well to heed as a light that shines in a dark place, until the day dawns and the morning star rises in your hearts" (2 Peter 1:19).

What does the apostle Peter mean when he speaks of the prophetic word being "more sure"? What is God's word "more sure" than? God's word is "more sure" than our own opinions. God's word is "more sure" than our own ideas. Prophecy clearly exposes Satan's deceptions.

We are not left to face the evil one's delusions without warning. Our loving Lord clearly reveals what is coming. In His powerful sermon on last-day signs, Jesus declared, "False christs and false prophets will arise and show great signs and wonders, so as to deceive, if possible, even the elect" (Matthew 24:24).

Notice that there are false christs and false prophets. What do they do? They perform false signs and wonders. These are counterfeit miracles. Ours is a generation in which seeing is supposedly believing. Experience is the supposed test of truth. Satan is conditioning the minds of millions to receive a counterfeit religious experience and be deceived by an emotional form of religion. False healing, miracles, and tongues will be part of his strategy.

Revelation tells us that "he performs great signs [miracles], so that he even makes fire come down from heaven on earth in the sight of men. And he deceives those who dwell on the earth by those signs he was granted to do in the sight of the beast" (Revelation 13:13, 14).

Mark this point carefully: the agency Satan uses to deceive many people in earth's final hours is miracles. Did you notice the statement, "He even makes fire come down from heaven"? Fire is a symbol of the glory, presence, and power of God through the Holy Spirit.

God pours out His genuine Spirit, which leads men and women to seek Him in sincere repentance for their sins and to receive a new revelation of His will for their lives. Using a false religious excitement, Satan pours out his counterfeit spirit of signs, wonders, and miracles to deceive.

This false religious excitement will swell to a great worldwide movement. At a time of international crisis, it will sweep the world. "They are the spirits of demons, performing signs, which go out to the kings of the earth and of the whole world, to gather them to the battle of that great day of God Almighty" (Revelation 16:14).

Through miraculous signs and wonders the devil will create a false religious excitement. He will attempt to take the minds of millions captive through this false revival.

Ellen White describes this counterfeit revival in *The Great Controversy.*

Before the final visitation of God's judgments upon earth there will be among the people of the Lord such a revival of primitive godliness as has not been witnessed since apostolic times. The Spirit and power of God will be poured out upon His children. . . . The enemy of souls desires to hinder this work; and before the time for such a movement shall come, he will endeavor to prevent it by introducing a counterfeit. In those churches which he can bring under his deceptive power he will make it appear God's special blessing is poured out; there will be manifest what is thought to be great religious interest. Multitudes will exult that God is working miraculously for them, when the work is that of another spirit. Under a religious guise, Satan will seek to extend his influence over the Christian world (p. 464).

Let's analyze this statement carefully.

- God is planning to send a mighty revival to His church at the end time.
- His Holy Spirit will be poured out powerfully.
- The enemy desires to hinder the latter rain and will introduce a counterfeit revival.
- Under a religious guise, Satan will deceive the world.

The last great deception of Satan will not come from secular humanism. It will be a religious deception. The stage is being set today. Crisis after crisis have rapidly affected our world. Terrorist attacks, natural disaster, political turmoil, and financial uncertainty have sobered ordinary people. People are looking for answers. Could it be that the devil will introduce a false religious revival to deceive millions? Wouldn't it be just like the devil to attack in an area most people are not expecting? If the devil could stir up a false religious excitement as a counterfeit to the genuine revival of the Holy Spirit in latter rain power, he will have accomplished his purpose.

Writing with prophetic insight, Ellen White confirms this technique: "Through the agency of spiritualism, miracles will be wrought, the sick will be healed, and many undeniable wonders will be performed" (*The Great Controversy*, p. 588).

Let's pause for a moment and remember, God can and will work miracles in the last days. Not all miracles are false miracles. Our God is all powerful. He will work mightily at the end time. But if God will work genuine miracles and Satan will work counterfeit miracles, how will we tell the difference? We will not be able to tell by looking at the miracle. The true and counterfeit miracles may look the same. At first glance they may be very, very similar.

Jesus provides the key to understanding how to determine between a true and counterfeit religious experience. "Not everyone who says to me, 'Lord, Lord,' shall enter the kingdom of heaven, but he who does the will of My Father in heaven. Many will say to me in that day, 'Lord, Lord, have we not prophesied in Your name, cast out demons in Your name, and done many wonders in Your name?' And then I will declare to them, 'I never knew you; depart from Me, you who practice lawlessness!' " (Matthew 7:21–23).

This is quite amazing. They did all these things—prophesy, cast out demons, and work wonders in Jesus' name. Nevertheless, Jesus declares, "I never knew you." He never knew them even when they were doing these mighty works in His name. Why not? To them, signs and wonders were more important than doing His will. To them, miracles were more important than a heart to know truth. To them, the outer appearance was more important than the inner reality. Emotionalism was more important than obedience.

Beware of any so-called religious revival that minimizes the teachings of God's Word, downplays doing God's will, and dismisses the importance of obedience. Beware of any so-called religious revival that is more interested in feeling good than being good.

Before the Holy Spirit fell on the disciples at Pentecost, they met in the upper room. They opened their hearts to God in earnest prayer. They repented of their sins. They confessed their faults. They committed their lives to obeying God. They were passionate about living for Jesus and sharing His love with others.

The Holy Spirit is longing to do something deep within the fabric of our being. He is longing to change us within. He desires to fill our hearts with the glory of His presence. The strange fires of emotionalism won't do. They are like a temporary fix but will leave our souls barren.

Would you like to seek the outpouring of the genuine Spirit of God on your life right now? Why not pray this prayer, asking the Holy Spirit to guide you?

Breathe on me, Breath of God.
Fill me with life anew,
That I may love what Thou doest love
And do what Thou wouldst do.

My Personal Application

Prayer is the breath of revival, but Bible study is its heart. All great revivals throughout history have been rooted in the Word of God. Revival without Bible study is soon reduced to emotionalism or some form of fanaticism. The Word of God provides the very foundation for revival. This week begin reading the Gospel of John. As you read each chapter, use the VIM principle.

V—Visualize the story in John's Gospel that you are reading and picture the scene in your mind. Attempt to grasp each detail of the story.

I—Identify with each character in the story. Ask questions such as How would I feel if I were the character in the story? For example, how would I feel if I were the woman with the issue of blood, the demoniac, the blind man, Nicodemus, the woman at the well, etc.? What thoughts would be running through my mind?

M—Meditate upon the story and ask these questions: How does this story apply to my life? What is God saying to me about the story? What lesson is He teaching me? Accept those lessons by faith and apply them to your life.

This week, read the following Bible passages and apply them to your life using the VIM principle.

- John 3:1–21   • John 4:1–26   • John 6: 1–4

CHAPTER FIVE

The Promised Revival

My wife and I lived in England for a number of years. We often spent Sunday afternoons in London visiting the historic sites. London is one of the most fascinating cities in the world with its magnificent Houses of Parliament, Westminster Abbey, Big Ben Clock Tower, and the world renowned London Bridge.

The story is told of a poverty stricken beggar who sat at the end of the London Bridge many years ago scraping away wretchedly on an old violin. The poor old man was futilely attempting to solicit a few pennies from passersby. But no one seemed to care about the old man's music, if you could call it music. The beggar's sad countenance revealed the sadness of his heart.

A well-dressed stranger passed, but suddenly halted; then he returned and listened to the old man, whose weary eyes searched his face for a trace of charity. But instead of offering the hoped-for penny, the stranger asked for his violin. He would help him out with a tune.

The stiff, numb fingers gently passed over the old instrument. The skilled hands carefully tuned the instrument and began to play a magnificent melody. Soon people stopped to listen. The crowd was small at first; then it grew larger. The music was irresistible.

A dense crowd now thronged the end of the London Bridge and stopped traffic. One silver coin after another was dropped into the old man's open violin case. Sweet and rapturous melody had replaced the weary scraping. And word passed through the crowd, "It is the hand of the master. It's Paganini playing on the old beggar's violin."

God longs for each of us to respond as did that old violin in the hands of the master. Then our lives will be filled with heavenly music. When the Holy Spirit takes total control of us, He will do amazing things. As an instrument in the Master's hands, the Spirit will do more through our lives than we can possibly imagine.

A last-day revival

The Bible predicts that there will be a mighty spiritual revival in the last days. The Holy Spirit will be poured out in Pentecostal power. The gospel will be proclaimed rapidly all over the world. Note these two powerful promises: "This gospel of the kingdom will be preached in all the world as a witness to all the nations, and then the end will come" (Matthew 24:14). "He will finish the work and cut it short in righteousness, because the Lord will make a short work upon the earth" (Romans 9:28). The gospel will be preached in all the world. God will work rapidly to finish His work.

The devil understands these prophecies, so before the coming of Jesus at the end time, he will work with all of his power. He will introduce his greatest deceptions. Through a counterfeit religious revival of signs, wonders, and miracles, the devil will mislead millions. But unusual power from beneath will call for mighty power from above. Satan will work—but God will work much more powerfully.

The last book of the Bible describes God's final revelation of glory in these words: "After these things I saw another angel coming down from heaven, having great authority, and the earth was illuminated with His glory" (Revelation 18:1).

In this last great revival, the Holy Spirit will be poured out in full power. The gospel will spread quickly around the world. Multitudes will respond to the preaching of God's Word. Thousands will share the words of life with their neighbors and find responsive hearts waiting to receive the truth.

The Bible refers to this mighty revival as the outpouring of the latter rain. The terms *early rain* and *latter rain* refer to part of the agriculture cycle of Israel. The early rain watered the seed that had been planted and helped it germinate. The latter rain fell at the end of the agricultural cycle to ripen the grain and bring it to harvest. Without the latter rain there would be no final harvest. The latter rain is one of the Bible's symbols for the outpouring of the Holy Spirit in the last days. The Holy Spirit empowers God's people to complete the task of preaching the gospel to the entire world before Jesus comes.

The apostle James puts it this way: "Be patient, brethren, until the coming of the Lord. See how the farmer waits for the precious fruit of the earth, waiting patiently for it until it receives the early and latter rain. You also be patient. Establish your hearts, for the coming of the Lord is at hand" (James 5:7, 8).

The Old Testament prophet Joel adds this promise: "Be glad then, you children of Zion, and rejoice in the LORD your God; for He has given you the former rain faithfully, and He will cause the rain to come down for you—the former rain, and the latter rain" (Joel 2:23).

Historically, the former or early rain fell at Pentecost. In one day, three thousand converts were baptized in a single place. God's Word says that this result is moderate in comparison to what is coming. If I saw three thousand people baptized on one day in one place in North America, I don't think I would call that a "moderate" outpouring of the Spirit. How about you? But the point here is that the early rain is moderate in comparison to what is coming in the latter rain.

We can expect the Holy Spirit to do some absolutely incredible things at the end time. We know that the outpouring of God's Spirit to finish the gospel work on earth will be far more powerful than anything God's church has ever seen before.

Pentecost will be repeated on a grander, larger scale. Ellen White explains: "The work will be similar to that of the Day of Pentecost. As the 'former rain' was given, in the outpouring of the Holy Spirit at the opening of the gospel, to cause the upspringing of the precious seed, so the 'latter rain' will be given at its close for the ripening of the harvest" (*The Great Controversy,* p. 611).

The passage continues with this powerful statement:

The great work of the gospel is not to close with less manifestation of the power of God than marked its opening. The prophecies which were fulfilled in the outpouring of the former rain at the opening of the gospel are again to be fulfilled in the latter rain at its close. . . .

Servants of God, with their faces lighted up and shining with holy consecration, will hasten from place to place to proclaim the message from heaven. By thousands of voices, all over the earth, the warning will be given. Miracles will be wrought, the sick will be healed, and signs and wonders will follow the believers (pp. 611, 612).

What a thrill to be living at a time when God desires to pour out all of Heaven's power in the closing work. What a privilege to be a channel for the outpouring of the Holy Spirit.

If we see the false manifestations of Satan in counterfeit revivals all around us, shouldn't we long for the genuine manifestation of the Holy Spirit in the latter rain? Shouldn't we be seeking God to send us that true manifestation? It is one thing to recognize the counterfeit. It is another to receive the genuine gift of the Spirit.

It is possible to become so focused on the counterfeit that we fail to recognize what God longs to do through His people today. It is possible to become so fearful of the false that we miss seeking for the showers of the latter rain in our own lives.

Do you long for the genuine outpouring of the Holy Spirit in your own life and in the life of the church? It is only as God's Spirit is poured out that the gospel message will go to the ends of the earth. The Old Testament prophet Zechariah proclaims that it is " 'not by might, nor by power, but by My

Spirit,' says the LORD of hosts" (Zechariah 4:6) that the work will be finished on earth.

What is holding back the coming revival? What barriers keep the latter rain from falling? What are Heaven's prerequisites for receiving this "latter rain" power of the Spirit? Why hasn't God poured out His Holy Spirit in all of its fullness yet? What is Heaven waiting for?

There is nothing more important for us personally or for the church as a whole than seeking the outpouring of the Holy Spirit in a heaven-sent revival. "A revival of true godliness among us is the greatest and most urgent of all of our needs. To seek this should be our first work" (*Selected Messages*, bk. 1, p. 121).

Meeting Heaven's conditions for revival and the outpouring of the Holy Spirit in latter rain power is our top priority. Heaven has much more to offer us than we could possibly imagine.

LeRoy E. Froom reported that "the bankers of Scotland are said to have 40,000,000 pounds in unclaimed deposits" (*The Coming of the Comforter*, p. 203.) Depending on the fluctuating exchange rates, this could be a whopping seventy to eighty million dollars unclaimed in one small country. It seems difficult to believe, but the riches of all heaven await our demand and reception. We need not wait for others to claim them. Oh the tragedy of our poverty! Do we fail to claim the unlimited resources the Holy Spirit holds for us?

Prerequisites for receiving the latter rain

Let's study some of God's prerequisites for receiving the

fullness of the Holy Spirit. If we want to receive latter rain power, here is what God's Word says.

1. The first prerequisite to receiving the Holy Spirit is to ask God.

"Ask the Lord for rain in the time of the latter rain" (Zechariah 10:1). God's messenger to His last-day church adds, "We should pray as earnestly for the descent of the Holy Spirit as the disciples prayed on the day of Pentecost" (*Review and Herald,* August 25, 1896).

Luke records the earnestness of the disciples' prayers at Pentecost. "These all continued with one accord in prayer and supplication, with the woman and Mary the mother of Jesus, and with His brothers" (Acts 1:14).

The disciples sensed they were powerless without the Spirit. They realized the task was just too daunting without the mighty outpouring of Heaven's power. Without the Spirit's presence in their lives in the fullness of power, they could not defeat the forces of hell.

The Holy Spirit will come in latter rain power only in answer to earnest prayer. We are counseled, "My brethren and sisters, plead for the Holy Spirit. God stands back of every promise He has made. With Bibles in your hands, say: 'I have done as Thou hast said, I present Thy promise, "Ask and it shall be given you; seek and you shall find; knock, and it shall be opened unto you" ' " (*Testimonies,* vol. 8, p. 23).

Are you seeking God daily for the baptism of the Holy Spirit? Are you praying for the outpouring of the Holy Spirit in your own life? Do you have a prayer group you are meeting with to seek God for the latter rain? Do you have two or three prayer partners you have covenanted with to pray for the outpouring of the Holy Spirit in your life and the life of the church? Remember that Jesus promised, "If you then, being evil, know how to give good gifts to your children, how much more will your heavenly Father give the Holy Spirit to those who ask Him!" (Luke 11:13).

Let's look at a second prerequisite for receiving the fullness of the Spirit.

2. The second prerequisite is an undivided heart.

You may ask, "What is an undivided heart?" An undivided heart is a heart totally dedicated to Jesus. It is a heart that is completely loyal to Him. It is a heart that longs to do God's will.

Jesus' life is the model of a life filled with the Spirit. Luke, chapter 3, describes the scene at His baptism. "While He prayed, the heaven was opened. And the Holy Spirit descended in bodily form like a dove upon Him" (Luke 3:21, 22).

In Luke 4:18, the Savior declares, "The Spirit of the LORD is upon Me." The Father's fascinating affirmation at Jesus' baptism opens new vistas of understanding regarding the reception of the Spirit. At the baptism, the Father spoke from heaven, declaring, "You are My beloved Son; in You I am well pleased" (Luke 3:22).

The Holy Spirit is poured out from heaven on those with whom the Father is well pleased. Jesus affirmed His heart's undivided loyalty in John 8:29 when He declared, "He who sent Me is with Me. The Father has not left Me alone, for I always do those things that please Him."

Jesus was totally committed to pleasing His Father. Nothing else in life mattered as much as doing the Father's will. The Father honored His Son's commitment by sending His Spirit without measure. God is willing to give you an undivided heart. Ask Him to teach you to live a life of absolute dependence upon Him.

When God has a group of people whose main desire is to please Him, He will then pour out His Spirit in abundance. As we pray for the outpouring of the Holy Spirit, our main focus is not some supernatural, spiritual power for ourselves. The Holy Spirit bears witness of Jesus. The Holy Spirit glorifies Jesus in our lives (John 15:26; 16:14). Jesus longs for us to come to Him with humble hearts, putting aside our own desires, saying, "Not as I will, but as You will" (Matthew 26:39).

Day by day Jesus allows various spiritual tests to come to us. Each test is an opportunity to discover what is in our hearts. He reveals things we never knew about ourselves. His great desire is that these tests will drive us to our knees praying, "Lord, I never knew that was inside of me. I never knew that was part of my nature. Please deliver me from the bondage of that specific habit or attitude. I willingly confess it and surrender it to You."

Connecting with the Source of power

God invites us to connect with the Source of all power. As we open our hearts to Him in prayer, our minds will be in harmony with His mind, our wills in harmony with His will, and our hearts one with His. An undivided, surrendered heart, seeking to please Him in all things, is a vital prerequisite for spiritual revival.

Did you read about the woman a number of years ago who bought a new refrigerator, and everything she put in it spoiled? The milk soured, the lettuce wilted, the fruit and vegetables rotted, and the ice cream melted. She couldn't figure out what was wrong. Everything seemed to be in working order. To her absolute surprise, she discovered the plug had come out of the socket. The refrigerator was not plugged in. It was not connected to the source of power. Similarly, spiritual power comes only when you are connected to the source of unlimited power.

Ellen White describes the results of having an undivided heart. "There is no limit to the usefulness of the one who, putting self aside, makes room for the working of the Holy Spirit upon his heart and lives a life wholly consecrated to God" (*Testimonies,* vol. 8, p. 19).

God has limitless plans for your life. There are no limits to what the Spirit can do in and through your life if you have an undivided heart and are wholly consecrated to God.

3. The third prerequisite for the reception of the Spirit is saturating our minds with the Word of God.

The same Holy Spirit who inspired the Bible inspires us as we read it. The same Holy Spirit who filled the lives of Bible writers as they wrote the sacred words of Scripture fills our lives as we read their words. The psalmist gives us a vital key to revival when he states, "My soul clings to the dust; revive me according to Your word" (Psalm 119:25). "My soul melts from heaviness; strengthen me according to Your word" (Psalm 119:28). "My soul faints for Your salvation, but I hope in Your word" (Psalm 119:81). "Plead my cause and redeem me; revive me according to Your word" (Psalm 119:154).

The psalmist clearly understood that the very foundation of revival is God's Word. The Holy Spirit transforms us as we meet Jesus in the words of Scripture. Facing the powerful temptations of the enemy in the wilderness temptation, Jesus emphatically declared, "Man shall not live by bread alone, but by every word that proceeds from the mouth of God" (Matthew 4:4). The Master added in John 6:63, "The words that I speak to you are spirit, and they are life."

The Holy Spirit flows through God's Word to fill up our lives. To be filled with the Spirit is to be filled with the Word of God. Spirit-filled lives are guided by the Word, instructed by the Word, and empowered by the Word. As we open the pages of Scripture, we are sanctified by the Word and transformed by the Word. When we absorb the teachings of God's Word, we give the Holy Spirit permission to fill our lives with His presence and power.

4. A fourth prerequisite in receiving the Holy Spirit in the fullness of His power is to put away all dissension between one another.

When the disciples were battling for the highest place, the Holy Spirit's power was limited. When they were arguing among themselves and harboring ill feelings toward one another, the Holy Spirit's power was limited. It is only by removing the road blocks of friction and conflict that the Spirit can be poured out upon our lives.

At Pentecost the disciples "were all with one accord in one place" (Acts 2:1). The New Testament Greek word translated "one accord" means "together." The disciples were not only physically together, but for the first time they were truly together in a harmonious unity. They still had their different personalities, but they were united in their commitment to one another. They were one in their desire to bring the gospel to the world.

Ellen White gives us this practical counsel: "Let Christians put away all dissension and give themselves to God for saving the lost. Let them ask in faith for the promised blessing, and it will come. The outpouring of the Spirit in the days of the apostles was 'the former rain,' and glorious was the result. But the latter rain will be more abundant" (*Testimonies*, vol. 8, p. 21).

Is there anything in your life that stands between you and someone else? Could it be that this wall is also a barrier to God in giving you the fullness of His power? Do you need to forgive someone who has hurt you? If you harbor bitterness, you allow that person to wound you again and again. Forgiveness is not justifying what another has done. It is releasing them from our condemnation when they do not deserve it because Christ released us from His condemnation when we do not deserve it. When we freely forgive, we open our hearts for the Holy Spirit to flow through us to others.

Corrie ten Boom survived one of Hitler's death camps. Her sister Betsy was not as fortunate. She died in the brutality and disease of the camp. After the war was over, Corrie traveled throughout her beloved Holland and Germany, sharing a message of reconciliation and peace. One evening after a presentation in a church in Germany, she saw him. The image of this short, stocky, steel-faced German prison guard was etched in her mind forever. His inhumane treatment of her sister Betsy had led to Betsy's death. But now this man stood before Corrie with his hand stretched out, asking, "Will you forgive me?" It took all of the grace possible to take this man's hand in hers, look him in the eye, and say, "Yes, I forgive you!" Corrie recognized this vital truth. The Holy Spirit cannot fill an unforgiving heart. The Holy Spirit and bitterness do not go together; like oil and water, they do not mix.

5. The fifth prerequisite for receiving the latter rain is active labor for others.

Remember, the outpouring of the Holy Spirit gave the disciples power to witness. God sends His power so that we can proclaim His message. He gives it so we can bless others.

Many people are looking to the future for some great outpouring of the Holy Spirit. But that outpouring can begin in our lives today. Now is the time to seek God for a spiritual revival. If this revival is to begin, it must begin within the heart of each of us.

Now is the time to share Jesus' love and grace with others. The more we share His love with others, the more the Holy Spirit fills us up with God's grace to share more.

The outpouring of the Holy Spirit in revival is linked to

our commitment to others. Because it is "more blessed to give than to receive," we are the ones most blessed as we share Jesus' love and truth. Ellen White makes this remarkable statement: "If coldness and indifference have crept over your spiritual senses, and your interest for those who are perishing in their sins is decreasing, it is time you were converted. Your best course will be to engage at once in personal efforts to save others. In blessing them, you will yourself be blessed" (*Review and Herald,* June 10, 1880).

Why would God pour out His Holy Spirit on us to witness to others if we have no interest in witnessing? Why would God empower us to share our faith if we are not interested in sharing it? The Holy Spirit testifies of Jesus. When we are interested in what the Holy Spirit is interested in, His power will be poured out on us in all of its fullness. It is now time to seek, with consecrated hearts, for the mighty power of God.

Receiving the latter rain calls for total surrender

God invites us to make His priorities, our priority. He urges us to place His will before our own. He appeals to us to "seek first the kingdom of God and His righteousness" in all aspects of our lives.

For five years, Mr. Van de Venter struggled with making a full decision to make Christ's call upon his life his own priority. Van de Venter was gradually becoming a recognized artist. But then he felt the Holy Spirit tugging at his heart. He was impressed to become an evangelist, but he resisted. Here is how he tells the story.

"For some time I had struggled between developing my

talents in the field of art and going into full-time evangelistic work. At last the pivoted hour of my life came, and I surrendered all. A new day was ushered into my life."

Pastor Van de Venter had a significant influence on Billy Graham. He often visited the Florida Bible Institute where Billy Graham was a student. Dr. Graham wrote, "One of the evangelists who influenced my early preaching was also a hymnist who wrote, 'I Surrender All'—the Rev. J. W. Van de Venter. He was a regular visitor at the Florida Bible Institute . . . in the late 1930's. We students loved this kind, deeply spiritual gentleman" (*101 More Hymn Stories,* p. 136).

"I Surrender All" reflects the depth of Pastor Van de Venter's spiritual commitment. As you thoughtfully read the words, why not rededicate your life in total surrender to the Christ of all power?

I Surrender All

All to Jesus I surrender,
All to Him I freely give;
I will ever love and trust Him,
In His presence daily live.

Chorus:
I surrender all,
I surrender all;
All to Thee, my blessed Savior,
I surrender all.

All to Jesus I surrender;
Humbly at His feet I bow,
Worldly pleasures all forsaken;
Take me Jesus, take me now.

All to Jesus I surrender;
Make me, Savior, wholly Thine;
Let me feel the Holy Spirit,
Truly know that thou art mine.

All to Jesus I surrender;
Lord, I give myself to Thee;
Fill me with Thy love and power;
Let Thy blessing fall on me.

Is the greatest desire of your life to be filled with His love and power? Do you long for His blessing right now? He is ready to pour out the abundant blessings of heaven upon you today. Why not bow your head and pray, "Jesus, I surrender all. I give all You ask and by faith receive all You have promised. Lord, You have promised acceptance, forgiveness, redemption, deliverance, adoption, hope, and power. By faith I claim Your promises at this very moment and believe the Holy Spirit's blessings are mine at this very moment. In Jesus' name, Amen."

My Personal Application

In revival, the Holy Spirit changes our thinking processes. He does a new thing in our lives. There is a new spiritual awakening in our hearts. Spiritual longings fill our souls. We have a hunger for the things of God. How does spiritual revival occur? How are we changed to be more like Jesus? The apostle Paul puts it this way: "We all, with unveiled face, beholding as in a mirror the glory of the Lord, are being transformed into the same image from glory to glory, just as by the Spirit of the Lord" (2 Corinthians 3:18). The apostle James adds that we are transformed by the "implanted word" (James 1:21). The apostle Peter declares that we are partakers of the divine nature through God's "exceedingly great and precious promises" (2 Peter 1:4).

As we come in contact with Jesus in His Word, we are transformed. As we meditate upon Jesus in His Word, revival fires are lit in our own hearts. This week enter into a fast for the next seven days. Fast from all television and DVD movies and spend thirty minutes each morning reading the Gospel of John and thirty minutes each evening reading *The Desire of Ages*.

"It would be well for us to spend a thoughtful hour each day in contemplation of the life of Christ. We should take it point by point, and let the imagination grasp each scene, especially the closing ones" (*The Desire of Ages*, p. 83).

My Commitment

❑ *This week I choose to fast from media entertainment to focus especially on my personal spiritual devotional life.*

CHAPTER SIX

Evangelism and Revival

Their fear was gone. It danced away like a fading shadow. Their dark night of gloom was over. Morning had come. Faith filled their hearts. They no longer cowered fearfully in the upper room. They were filled with faith. Hope overflowed in their hearts. One glimpse of their resurrected Lord had changed their lives. Jesus gave them a new reason for living. He gave them what has come to be known as the Great Commission, "Go into all the world and preach the gospel to every creature" (Mark 16:15).

Now they were clinging to the great promise. For without the great promise, they could not fulfill the Great Commission. Imagine that you were in the upper room with the disciples two thousand years ago. The integrity of God's word is at stake. His reputation is on the line. The honor of God's throne depends on the fulfillment of His promise.

The great promise

In spite of overwhelming obstacles and insurmountable odds, the disciples clung to that precious promise. "Being assembled together with them, He commanded them not to depart from Jerusalem, but to wait for the Promise of the Father, 'which,' He said, 'you have heard from Me. . . . But you shall receive power when the Holy Spirit has come upon you; and you shall be witnesses to Me in Jerusalem, and in all Judea and Samaria, and to the end of the earth' " (Acts 1:4–8).

The disciples clung to Jesus' word. They trusted the Savior's promise. They were confident that if they fulfilled the conditions, He would fulfill His word. They waited. They confessed their sins. They prayed. They believed. And Heaven answered. The Holy Spirit was poured out in abundant measure on the Day of Pentecost (Acts 2:1–4).

The outpouring of the Spirit on the Day of Pentecost was not simply because the disciples had met the conditions. Certainly the Holy Spirit would not have been poured out if they had not met the conditions, but meeting the conditions of receiving the Spirit, in itself, was not enough.

The Holy Spirit was poured out on the Day of Pentecost as a signal to the early church that Jesus' sacrifice was accepted by the Father in the heavenly sanctuary. Luke makes this clear in Acts 2. "This Jesus God has raised up, of which we are all witnesses. Therefore being exalted to the right hand of God, and having received from the Father the promise of the Holy Spirit, He poured out this which you now see and hear" (Acts 2:32, 33).

The mighty outpouring of the Spirit on Pentecost was Heaven's gift, confirming the Father's acceptance of the magnificent sacrifice of Christ on Calvary's cross. The three thousand baptized that day were an eloquent testimony of the risen Christ's power to change lives. The fullness of the Spirit testified to the fullness of Jesus' power.

The disciples gathered in the upper room that day numbered 120. The challenge of reaching the world with the gospel seemed impossible. Our best population estimates for the Roman Empire during the first century are approximately 180 million.

Although there certainly were a few more Christians than those gathered in the upper room, the percentage of Christians to the world population was infinitesimal. For example, if we use the 120 figure, there would have been one Christian to each 1.4 million people in the world.

In comparison, today we have approximately one Adventist to every 422 people in the world. In an age of Roman military might and materialism, Greek philosophy, and pagan religion, their task would have appeared much more daunting than ours.

These early believers did not have mass media, radio, television, or the Internet. They did not have the social media network such as Facebook, Twitter, or text messaging. They did not have a network of satellite television stations. They did not have seminaries, publishing houses, and a worldwide hospital system. They did not have a worldwide church organization; but this they had—the fullness of the Spirit. They had Jesus' promise that through the outpouring of His Holy Spirit, they would reach the entire world with His message of love and truth.

Explosive growth in Acts

The results were astounding! Journey with me through the book of Acts and catch the inspiration as we stand back in awe at the moving of the Holy Spirit. The book of Acts reveals what God can do in a very short time through consecrated men and women who believe His promise and act upon His Word.

When the disciples woke up on the Day of Pentecost, they had no idea that the church would add three thousand new members that very day. Acts 2:41 records, "Then those who gladly received his word were baptized; and that day about three thousand souls were added to them." And this was just the beginning. Acts 4:4 adds, "However, many of those who heard the word believed; and the number of the men came to be about five thousand."

You will notice that the text says the number of men was five thousand. If we add women and children, the numbers dramatically increase. Most estimates are that by the time of Acts 4, the Christian church numbered fifteen to twenty thousand. In just a few short weeks, the church membership exploded. The record of this amazing phenomenon continues in Acts 6:7, "Then the word of God spread, and the number of the disciples multiplied greatly in Jerusalem, and a great many of the priests were obedient to the faith."

As the disciples preached under the influence of the Holy Spirit, the risen Christ touched the hearts of many Jewish religious leaders. Many of them, along with their congregations, accepted this new faith. The impact of the New Testament church continued to increase in remarkable ways.

One Roman writer put it this way: "You are everywhere. You are in our armies, you are in our navies, our senate and market places," referring to the widespread reach of Christianity.

Pliny the Younger, governor of the Roman province of Bithynia on the north coast of modern Turkey, wrote to Emperor Trajan around A.D. 110. Pliny's statement is significant because it was written nearly eighty years after the Crucifixion. Pliny described the official trials he was conducting to find and execute Christians. He stated, "Many of every age, of every social class, even of both sexes, are being called to trial and will be called. Nor cities alone, but villages in even rural areas have been invaded by the infection of this superstition [Christianity]" (*Epistulae* 10.96, gjr).

This quote from Pliny shows us that in a remote province, Christianity had invaded every level of society in a few generations. Ninety years later, around A.D. 200, Tertullian, a Roman lawyer turned Christian, wrote a defiant letter to the Roman magistrates defending Christianity. He boasted that "nearly all the citizens of all the cities are Christians" (*Apologeticus* 37.8, gjr). The story of the book of Acts is the story of remarkable growth of the Christian church in a very short period of time.

With the conversion of the apostle Paul, recorded in Acts 9, the Christian church added the most powerful evangelist of his time. Through the ministry of the Holy Spirit, Paul raised up churches throughout Asia Minor and the Mediterranean world.

Acts 10 tells how through a vision Peter received while praying God broke down his barriers of prejudice between Jew and Gentile. Through the conversion of Cornelius, the door was now opened for the tens of thousands of Gentiles to enter the Christian church.

The book of Acts moves as a glorious symphony to a great crescendo. With the conversion of Cornelius, the Holy Spirit led these early believers beyond the confines of Judaism. As tens of thousands of Gentiles became Christians, churches were established. The Holy Spirit led each member to share his or her faith with others. Churches were established. Rather than building large churches in a few geographical centers, the disciples planted churches in communities throughout the Mediterranean world.

The New Testament was a church-planting movement. The record states, "Then the churches throughout all Judea, Galilee, and Samaria had peace and were edified. And walking in the fear of the Lord and in the comfort of the Holy Spirit, they were multiplied" (Acts 9:31). Did you notice the significance of the passages "the churches . . . were edified" and "multiplied." Genuine revival edifies, or builds up, the church in Christ and in His word. It also leads to multiplication of His church and to evangelistic outreach.

There is no genuine revival without a corresponding evangelistic outreach. Revival, without witnessing, results in either self-righteousness or spiritual complacency. Revival in the book of Acts resulted in a passion to share Jesus' love with others. This is why Acts 12:24 records, "The word of God grew and multiplied." The Word of God implanted in our hearts creates revival, and that Word overflows from our hearts in witness.

The last section of the book of Acts focuses primarily on the moving of the Holy Spirit through Paul to establish new congregations such as Philippi, Colossae, and Ephesus. By the time the book of Acts concludes, Paul could testify to the church at Colossae that the gospel had been preached to every creature under heaven (Colossians 1:23). The apostle shares the New Testament church's passion for evangelism in these words regarding their resurrected Lord. "Him we preach, warning every man and teaching every man in all wisdom, that we may present every man perfect in Christ Jesus. To this end I also labor, striving according to His working which works in me mightily" (Colossians 1:28, 29).

"As these messengers of the cross went forth to proclaim the gospel, there was such a revelation of the glory of God as had never before been witnessed by mortal man. By the co-operation of the divine Spirit, the apostles did a work that shook the world. To every nation was the gospel carried in a single generation" (*The Acts of Apostles,* p. 593).

What a change. What a transformation. What a miracle. These early disciples who numbered around 120 on the Day of Pentecost now, according to the best estimates of Christian historians, numbered over one million. The ratio of Christians to world population had dramatically changed in thirty years.

Through the miracle-working power of the Holy Spirit, the New Testament church absolutely exploded in growth. Their success was nothing short of phenomenal. It was possible only because of the mighty outpouring of the Holy Spirit. The need was great. The time was right. They met the conditions, and God fulfilled His promise.

Notice the striking similarities between the New Testament Christian church and the Advent movement. These early

Christians believed that Jesus was going to set up His kingdom in the first century. They misunderstood the Old Testament prophecies.

A few days before the Cross, James and John influenced their mother to ask Jesus to give them a prominent place in His new kingdom. The disciples failed to understand the magnitude of Christ's mission. They were totally unprepared for the Cross.

The disappointment of Calvary in A.D. 31 led them to humility, confession, repentance, and deep soul searching. The Cross prepared them for Pentecost, trusting in the promise of their resurrected Lord. They looked beyond their tears and disappointments to the sanctuary above to receive the outpouring of the Holy Spirit in the early rain.

The latter rain and the Advent movement

Fast-forward two thousand years. It is the end time. The prophecies of Daniel and Revelation are approaching a glorious climax. Christ's last-day followers misunderstood Daniel 8:14: "For two thousand three hundred days; then the sanctuary shall be cleansed." They were convinced that the cleansing of sanctuary was the cleansing of the earth by fire. They believed that Jesus would come at the conclusion of the 2,300 days in 1844.

They confessed their sins and joyfully anticipated His return. Debts were paid. Potatoes were left in the field without being harvested. Wrongs were righted. Families gathered, waiting for the coming of Jesus. The hope of His return burned brightly in their hearts. But like these early disciples, they, too, were bitterly disappointed. Their hopes were dashed. Their dreams were crushed. And like those first-century disciples, they sought God for an explanation about the disappointment. They knew that God had an answer to their dilemma. He could solve the mystery of their disappointment.

Ellen White wrote,

> We must be much in prayer if we would make progress in the divine life. When the message of truth was first proclaimed, how much we prayed. How often was the voice of intercession heard in the chamber, in the barn, in the orchard, or the grove. Frequently we spent hours in earnest prayer, two or three together claiming the promise; often the sound of weeping was heard and then the voice of thanksgiving and the song of praise. Now the day of God is nearer than when we first believed, and we should be more earnest, more zealous, and fervent than in those early days. Our perils are greater now than then. Souls are more hardened. We need now to be imbued with the spirit of Christ, and we should not rest until we receive it (*Testimonies,* vol. 5, pp. 161, 162).

Like the first-century followers of the Master, these early Adventists waited upon the Lord. God answered their prayers. He opened up to their understanding the truth about the judgment and the heavenly sanctuary. The sanctuary to be cleansed was not on earth, but in heaven. In the Old Testament, the Day of Atonement, or cleansing of the earthly sanctuary, was a day of final judgment.

In these last days of earth's history, Jesus, our great High Priest, invites us to open our hearts to Him in light of the judgment hour. Revelation's last-day message to this world declares, "Fear God and give glory to Him, for the hour of His judgment has come; and worship Him who made heaven and earth, the sea and the springs of water" (Revelation 14:7). In harmony with the heavenly sanctuary, our hearts are to be cleansed of anything that stands between us and Jesus. As we seek Jesus and receive the Holy Spirit's cleansing, the Spirit will fill us with latter-rain power to finish His work.

Pentecost repeated

The same Holy Spirit that was poured out on the New Testament believers to launch the church in Acts will be poured out more abundantly in the latter rain to finish the work of God on earth. God did the impossible in the first century, and He will do it again. God worked miracles then, and He will work miracles now.

Ellen White puts it this way: "All that the apostles did, every church member today is to do. And we are to work with as much more fervor, to be accompanied by the Holy Spirit in as much greater measure, as the increase of wickedness demands a more decided call to repentance" (*Review and Herald*, January 13, 1903).

The New Testament era was one of mighty miracles. The sick were healed. Demons were cast out. Tens of thousands were converted. Will this happen again in our day? Does God promise that in the mighty outpouring of the latter rain we will have a similar experience to the church in the book of Acts?

Here is a remarkable statement from the book *The Great Controversy:*

> The work will be similar to that of the Day of Pentecost. As the "former rain" was given, in the outpouring of the Holy Spirit at the opening of the gospel, to cause the upspringing of the precious seed, so the "latter rain" will be given at its close for the ripening of the harvest. . . .
>
> The great work of the gospel is not to close with less manifestation of the power of God than marked its opening (p. 611).

The greatest manifestation of the power of the Holy Spirit is promised for our day. God is ready to do amazing things. He is preparing to pour out His Holy Spirit without measure. Notice these clear Bible promises on the outpouring of the latter rain.

Zechariah 10:1—"Ask the LORD for rain in the time of the latter rain. The LORD will make flashing clouds; He will give them showers of rain, grass in the field for everyone."

Hosea 10:12—"Sow for yourselves righteousness; reap in mercy; break up your fallow ground, for it is time to seek the LORD, till He comes and rains righteousness on you."

Jeremiah 5:24—"They do not say in their heart, 'Let us now fear the LORD our God, who gives rain, both the former and the latter, in its season.' "

In agriculture there is a harvest cycle. In nature's cycle there is a time for sowing and a time for reaping. There is a time for planting, a time for seed to germinate, a time for crops to grow, and a time for the rains to bring the crops to harvest. God's plan of salvation also has a divine timetable. Jesus was born on time. Jesus was baptized on time. Jesus died on time. Jesus was resurrected on time. Jesus ascended to the Father on time. Jesus poured out the Holy Spirit in early rain power on time to launch the Christian church.

But now we are living in the time of the latter rain; the clock has struck the hour. The climax of history has come. This is the hour of the outpouring of the latter rain in all its fullness to prepare the church for the last proclamation of the gospel before the coming of Jesus. We are living at the time of the latter rain.

The dispensation in which we are now living is to be, to those that ask, the dispensation of the Holy Spirit. Ask for His blessing. It is time we were more intense in our devotion. To us is committed the arduous, but happy, glorious work of revealing Christ to those who are in darkness. We are called to proclaim the special truths for this time. For this assignment, the outpouring of the Spirit is essential. We should pray for it. The Lord expects us to ask Him. We have not been wholehearted in this work (*Testimonies to Ministers and Gospel Workers,* pp. 511, 512).

We are assured that all of God's biddings are enablings. Everything He asks us to do, He gives us power to do. The work of God on earth can never be finished without the power of the latter rain. All of heaven is waiting for God's people to open their hearts to the divine infilling of the Holy Spirit in Pentecostal power for the finishing of God's work on earth. God's end-time church has been given a special message and a special mission. God promises special power to proclaim the message and complete the mission.

When Napoleon led his armies into Egypt in 1799, his soldiers amassed on the great desert of Giza. They stood in awestruck wonder before the great pyramid of Cheops. As they stood there silently before those great monuments in stone, Napoleon cried out, "Soldiers, forty centuries look down upon you."

I would like to paraphrase Napoleon's statement, "We live at the crossroads of eternity. All of heaven is looking down upon us." The history of the ages is shining upon this final generation of Adventists. Could it be that God wants to do in each one of our lives "exceedingly abundantly above all that we ask or think" (Ephesians 3:20)?

Christ has given to the church a sacred charge. Every member should be a channel through which God can communicate to the world the treasures of His grace, the unsearchable riches of Christ. There is nothing that the Saviour desires so much as agents who will represent to the world His Spirit and His character. There is nothing that the world needs so much as the manifestation through humanity of the Saviour's love. All heaven is waiting for men and women through whom God can reveal the power of Christianity (*The Acts of the Apostles,* p. 600).

God longs to do amazing things through you. You can be a witness of His love in these last days. You can be a light in a darkened world. You can reveal His compassion to the people in your sphere of influence. He will open amazing doors of opportunity for you to share His last-day message with your family, friends, and neighbors. What a privilege! There is no higher privilege and no greater joy than being used of God to touch another's life for the kingdom of God.

This is our calling. This is our destiny. This is our opportunity. It is my prayer that the flame of revival will burn brightly in your heart so you can kindle the sparks of revival in the lives of others.

Would you like to say, "Jesus, I want to recommit my life to You today, asking You to fill me with Your Holy Spirit so I can be a mighty witness for You in the closing work"?

My Personal Application

The more we love Jesus, the more we desire to share His love with others. All true revival is based in prayer, centered in the Word of God, and focused on sharing Jesus' love with others. The revived heart is a witnessing heart. Ellen White puts it this way: "No sooner does one come to Christ than there is born in his heart a desire to make known to others what a precious friend he has found in Jesus; the saving and sanctifying truth cannot be shut up in his heart" (*Steps to Christ*, p. 78).

There is still another aspect of revival and witnessing. Witnessing is not only the result of revival, but witnessing leads to revival. Witnessing is one of God's means of reviving a spiritually complacent heart. *The Acts of the Apostles* testifies, "Strength to resist evil is best gained by aggressive service" (p. 105). Ellen White adds, "In order for us to develop a character like Christ's, we must share in His work" (*The Desire of Ages*, p. 142).

This week ask God to impress your heart with a specific ministry area in your local church where you can serve. What does God want you to do? How does He want you to be involved?

Why not fall on your knees and say, "Lord, I give You permission to use me in any way You wish to bless others and win souls for Your kingdom. Show me what You want me to do; whatever it is, by Your grace I choose to do it. I am open to serve You and use the gifts You have given me to bless others. Reveal Your will, and I will follow it."

CHAPTER SEVEN

Revival and a Finished Work

The figures are staggering. The task seems overwhelming. The mission before us appears, to all human reasoning, impossible. The world's population will reach seven billion sometime in 2011. Currently, there are over a billion people in both China and India. The continent of Africa has just topped the one billion mark. Of more than six billion people on the planet, only approximately 30 percent, or 2.2 billion, are Christian.

There are 1.5 billion Muslims, 1.1 billion secular agnostics and atheists, 900 million Hindus, and 376 million Buddhists, along with hundreds of other religious groups.

Although the Seventh-day Adventist Church is one of the fastest growing Christian denominations, baptizing about one million people each year, with 16.3 million members, we are approximately only 1 percent of all Christians and only a fraction of a percent of the world's population. This leads us to some thought-provoking questions.

How will the work of God on earth ever be finished?

Is it possible for the gospel in the context of the three angels' messages to circle the globe in a relatively short time?

What will give us the breakthrough in the proclamation of the gospel that we long for?

When will we see the fulfillment of Jesus words, "This gospel of the kingdom will be preached in all the world as a witness to all nations, and then the end will come" (Matthew 24:14)?

The mission is God's

Here is the key: The mission of reaching lost people with the "everlasting gospel" is His mission. It is not ours.

He invites us to cooperate with Him in finishing His work. God never asks us to do anything that He does not empower us to do. As we unite with Him in His mission of reaching a lost world, He promises to mightily pour out His Spirit to enable us to accomplish the seemingly impossible.

The promise of the Spirit

Before His ascension to heaven, Jesus made this promise to His earthly disciples: "I tell you the truth. It is to your advantage that I go away; for if I do not go away, the Helper will not come to you; but if I depart, I will send Him to you" (John 16:7).

This must have seemed like an incredible statement to the disciples. How could it be to their advantage that Jesus was leaving them? But He pledged to send in all of its fullness, with all of Heaven's power, the Third Person of the Godhead, the Holy Spirit.

The Master promised, "You shall receive power when the

Holy Spirit has come upon you; and you shall be witnesses to Me in Jerusalem, and in all Judea and Samaria, and to the end of the earth" (Acts 1:8).

Jesus' promise of the outpouring of the Holy Spirit was fulfilled at Pentecost. In one place, three thousand were baptized in a single day. The power of God worked so mightily that in one generation the gospel reached the far corners of the earth.

There are three aspects of Jesus' promise that I would like to explore with you. They are the all-encompassing nature of the promise, the all-embracing conditions of the promise, and the all-empowering results of the promise.

The all-encompassing nature of the promise

The story of the book of Acts is not the story of a few isolated individuals receiving the outpouring of the Holy Spirit here and there. It is the story of the church receiving the mighty outpouring of the Spirit.

The church sought the infilling of the Holy Spirit. The church prayed. The church opened its heart to the blessing of God. The church confessed. The church repented. The church committed itself to mission, and God answered from heaven.

Let's review that upper room prayer meeting recorded in Acts 1 and 2 once. "These all continued with one accord in prayer and supplication, with the women and Mary the mother of Jesus, and with His brothers. And in those days Peter stood up in the midst of the disciples (altogether the number of names was about one hundred and twenty)" (Acts 1:14, 15).

This fledgling church earnestly sought God in prayer. They prayed for the promised outpouring of the Holy Spirit. They recognized their insufficiency to reach the world with the story of their resurrected Lord.

As they prayed, confessing their sins, seeking God for power to proclaim His grace, the floodgates of heaven opened, and the rain of the Spirit poured down upon them.

Acts describes the scene this way: "And they were *all* filled with the Holy Spirit and began to speak with other tongues, as the Spirit gave them utterance" (Acts 2:4; emphasis added).

Notice carefully that the text says, "And they were *all* filled with the Holy Spirit."

Who were the "*all*" that were filled?

Not simply the disciples—all of those in the upper room—the one hundred and twenty believers.

When Peter quotes the fulfillment of Joel's prophecy, he declares,

> " 'And it shall come to pass in the last days, says God,
> That I will pour out My Spirit on *all* flesh;
> Your sons and your daughters shall prophesy,
> Your young men shall see visions,
> Your old men shall dream dreams.
> And on My menservants and on My maidservants,
> I will pour out My Spirit in those days' " (Acts 2:17, 18; emphasis added).

God has no respect of gender. The Holy Spirit will be poured out without measure on "your sons and your daughters." God has no respect of age. The Holy Spirit will be poured out without measure on the young and old. God has no respect of status. The Holy Spirit will even be poured out without measure on your menservants and maidservants.

In *The Acts of the Apostles,* Ellen White states,

> The lapse of time has wrought no change in Christ's parting promise to send the Holy Spirit as His representative. It is not because of any restriction on the part of God that the riches of His grace do not flow earthward to men. If the fulfillment of the promise is not seen as it might be, it is because the promise is not appreciated as it should be. If *all* were willing, *all* would be filled with the Spirit. Wherever the need of the Holy Spirit is a matter little thought of, there is seen spiritual drought, spiritual darkness, spiritual declension and death. Whenever minor matters occupy the attention, the divine power which is necessary for the growth and prosperity of the church, and which would bring all other blessings in its train, is lacking, though offered in infinite plenitude (p. 50; emphasis added).

Here is something broader and deeper than we may have previously grasped. Throughout the Old Testament, God poured out His Holy Spirit on individuals; but at Pentecost, He poured out His Holy Spirit on His church.

The church in Acts was a Spirit-filled church that reached the world with the gospel. God longs to do it again. He longs to pour His Spirit out on male and female, young and old, rich and poor, the educated and the uneducated, the literate and the illiterate.

The promise of the Spirit is for you. It is for me. It is for your church and conference, your union, your division, and the General Conference. The promise is all embracing. It is ours. We can claim it today. Jesus longs to fill us with the power of His Spirit. His promise is for this time, in this place, here and now. But this leads to two fundamental questions.

First, how can we personally receive this infilling of the Holy Spirit? Second, how can the church corporately receive the mighty outpouring of the Holy Spirit?

The all-encompassing conditions of the promise

There is one thing for certain: the outpouring of the Holy Spirit will not come without earnest, heartfelt intercession.

Luke records that the church in Acts "all continued with one accord in prayer" (Acts 1:14).

Ellen White adds, "We should pray as earnestly for the descent of the Holy Spirit as the disciples prayed on the day of Pentecost" (*Review and Herald,* August 25, 1896).

Zechariah the prophet echoes these sentiments with this admonition: "Ask the LORD for rain in the time of the latter rain" (Zechariah 10:1).

Jesus encourages us to seek the Spirit: "If you then, being evil, know how to give good gifts to your children, how much more will your heavenly Father give the Holy Spirit to those who ask Him!" (Luke 11:13).

"My brethren and sisters, plead for the Holy Spirit. God stands back of every promise He has made" (*Testimonies,* vol. 8, p. 23).

The reason God invites us to earnestly pray for the Holy

Spirit is not that He is unprepared to give us His Spirit but that we are unprepared to receive it. It is not that God is not longing to give us the Holy Spirit. It is that we do not long to receive it as much as He longs to give it. It is not that God is slow to pour out His Spirit in its fullness. It is, rather, that we have been slow in receiving the fullness of the Holy Spirit's power. It is not that God does not recognize our need of the Holy Spirit to finish His work. It is, rather, that we do not fully recognize our need.

Is it possible that, at times, we have substituted human plans, methods, and organization, as important as they are, for the power of the Holy Spirit?

Listen to this powerful statement from the pen of inspiration, "Do not rest satisfied that in the ordinary course of the season, rain will fall. Ask for it. . . . We must seek His favors with the whole heart if the showers of grace are to come to us" (*Review and Herald*, March 2, 1897).

Biblical conditions for revival

One of the biblical conditions of revival is heartfelt intercession. God grants the Holy Spirit to those who seek Him. Another essential element of revival is confession of all known sin. When the disciples met together in the upper room, they put "away all differences, all desire for the supremacy, they came close together in Christian fellowship. They drew nearer and nearer to God, and as they did this they realized what a privilege had been theirs in being permitted to associate so closely with Christ. Sadness filled their hearts as they thought of how many times they had grieved Him by their slowness of comprehension, their failure to understand the lessons that, for their good, He was trying to teach them" (*The Acts of the Apostles,* p. 37).

Ellen White makes it plain that "[t]hese days of preparation were days of deep heart searching" (*The Acts of Apostles,* p. 37). Their confessions mingled with tears. The disciples recognized that their pride and desire for the supremacy had limited what Jesus desired to do for them. They opened their hearts to the cleansing power of the Holy Spirit. They longed to fully experience Jesus' love in their lives. They longed to reflect His loving character to others. Christ was everything to them. They now understood the meaning of His sacrifice on the cross more fully. They grasped the significance of salvation through His grace. Filled with His love, charmed by His grace, and armed with His resurrection power, they were able to turn the world upside down through the infilling of His Holy Spirit.

God longs to pour out His Spirit on His church again. He longs to break our hearts with His love, transform us through His grace, and fill us with His power.

In 1888, two young preachers, A. T. Jones and E. J. Waggoner, presented a series of messages at the Minneapolis, Minnesota, General Conference Session. As they presented the "matchless charms of Christ," the reaction of the delegates was mixed. Some felt that these were the most precious messages they had ever heard. They recommitted their lives to Jesus and entered into a deeper experience with Him than ever before. Others argued that Adventists had always preached Jesus and that Elders Jones and Waggoner were emphasizing grace at the expense of the law. They opposed this "new teaching" and felt that it would lead to a lack of emphasis on the law of God.

Ellen White weighed in heavily on this topic. In 1892, she wrote, "The loud cry of the third angel has already begun in the revelation of the righteousness of Christ, the sin-pardoning Redeemer. This is the beginning of the light of the angel whose glory shall fill the whole earth" (*Review and Herald,* November 22, 1892).

In the four years following that General Conference session in Minneapolis, the message of righteousness by faith in the context of the three angels' messages to prepare a people for the coming of Jesus was so compelling that Ellen White could say that the "Loud Cry" had already begun. The Adventist Church was aroused. The spiritual life of God's people that had become dormant was revitalized. There was a spiritual awakening.

What in the message of 1888 is so compelling, so life changing, so powerful? Simply put, it is this: Jesus Christ longs to save us more than we long to be saved. Jesus came to redeem us from both the penalty and power of sin. This message of His all-sufficient, saving grace is an urgent appeal to confession, repentance, and total dependence on Jesus. It is a call away from self-sufficiency, a dependence on human works or accomplishments.

"What is justification by faith? It is the work of God in laying the glory of man in the dust, and doing for man that which it is not in his power to do for himself. When men see their own nothingness, they are prepared to be clothed with the righteousness of Christ" (*The Faith I Live By,* p. 111).

It is this message of the all-sufficiency of Jesus that will break our hearts, lead us to repentance, and open our hearts to receive His life-transforming power. When God has a people totally committed to Jesus, surrendered to do His will, revealing His loving character to the world, He will pour out His Spirit in Pentecostal power for the finishing of His work.

At the 1973 Annual Council of the Seventh-day Adventist Church, with delegates from around the world present, Elder Robert Pierson, president of the General Conference, appealed to the delegates assembled at the world headquarters in Washington, D.C., to seek a renewed experience with Christ in personal spiritual revival. The Holy Spirit's influence was felt in a marked way. Delegates sought God on their knees. They honestly confessed their sins. They studied God's Word together. The 1973 Annual Council resulted in one of the most pointed appeals on revival ever called for by the church.

It states,

The message to Laodicea involves a personal relationship to Jesus Christ that will produce a quality people, a conquering people, a people who, in Christ's own words, will conquer "as I myself conquered" (Revelation 3:21 RSV). This message will produce a people whom God can set forth without embarrassment as exhibits of those who "keep the commandments of God and the faith of Jesus" (Revelation 14:12 RSV), a people who have learned by experience that all goodness is a result of being sustained by divine power. Such people can be entrusted with special power because they will use it the way Jesus used power; indeed, in all aspects of life they will reflect the character of Jesus (Annual Council appeal, October 18, 1973).

The delegates at the 1973 Annual Council were deeply moved by this appeal. It became the basis of study at pastors' meetings and local churches. It reflected the New Testament emphasis on prayer, Bible study, confession of all known sin, repentance, and witnessing. Revival in every age is always the result of a passionate commitment to Jesus. The spiritual principles that led to revival in the first century lead to revival in every generation. When Evan Roberts of the Welsh Revival was asked, "What are the steps to a mighty spiritual revival?" he responded, "It is really quite simple."

Evan Roberts's steps to spiritual revival

1. Seek God and confess all known sin. **Pray.**
2. Deal with and get rid of anything doubtful in your life. **Commit.**
3. Be ready to obey the Spirit instantly. **Listen.**
4. Confess Christ publicly. **Witness.**

Seek God in prayer. Earnestly intercede. Pray daily for a fresh anointing of the Holy Spirit. Consecrate everything you have and are to God. Listen to the Holy Spirit's voice in God's Word, and as God reveals truth, be ready to follow it immediately. Share what God is doing in your life with others.

Witnessing and the latter rain

Do not hesitate in proclaiming His love and grace to those God brings into your life. Witnessing Christians are growing Christians. The more we are filled with the Holy Spirit, the more we long to share the Christ who has changed our own lives. The more we are actively involved in sharing Jesus with others, the more the Holy Spirit will fill us to share more of Jesus' love.

Why would God pour out His Spirit in latter rain power to finish His work if the majority of the church had little or no interest in witnessing? If the latter rain, the fullness of the Holy Spirit's power, is to empower the church to reach the world with God's end-time message, why would God give us the latter rain if we have a complacent, lukewarm attitude toward reaching lost people? The fullness of the Holy Spirit's power will be poured out on a praying, totally committed, unified, witnessing church.

Ellen White summarizes it beautifully in these words: "Let Christians put away all dissension and give themselves to God for the saving of the lost. Let them ask in faith for the promised blessing, and it will come" (*Testimonies*, vol. 8, p. 21).

Self-centeredness, pride, all striving for supremacy, competition between ministries and denominational entities limits what God can do through us.

- His power will be unleashed when we allow Him to reign supreme in our lives. His power will be unleashed as we are willing to give Him the glory for whatever He accomplishes through us.

- His power will be unleashed as we love the lost as He loves the lost.
- His power will be unleashed when advancing His kingdom is more important to us than building our own kingdom.
- His power will be unleashed when His honor is more important than our own. His power will be unleashed when the things that matter to us the most are the things that matter to Him the most.
- His power will be unleashed when the things that are on our minds are the things that are on His mind.

The good news is that He will have a final generation of committed men and women whom He uses to complete His mission on earth.

The all-empowering results of the promise

Bible prophecy reveals there will be a mighty outpouring of the Holy Spirit just before our Lord returns. According to Revelation 18:1, "The earth [will be] illuminated with [God's] glory."

God will triumph over all of the powers of evil. The forces of hell will not hinder the fulfillment of His plan. The gospel will go to the ends of the earth. Hundreds of thousands will accept Jesus and His truth in the final hours of earth's history.

Evil will not have the last word—God will.
Disease will not have the last word—God will.
Poverty will not have the last word—God will.
Sickness will not have the last word—God will.

Suffering will not have the last word—God will.
Man will not have the last word—God will.

God's plan, God's people, God's church will be triumphant at last.

Servants of God, with their faces lighted up and shining with holy consecration, will hasten from place to place to proclaim the message from heaven. By thousands of voices, all over the earth, the warning will be given. Miracles will be wrought, the sick will be healed, and signs and wonders will follow the believers. . . .

The message will be carried not so much by argument as by the deep conviction of the Spirit of God (*The Great Controversy*, p. 612).

The work of God on earth will be finished. The mission will be accomplished. The task will be complete. Jesus will come to deliver His people. He will come as the Mighty Deliverer.

He will come as King of kings and Lord of lords. He will come as the victorious Conqueror. He will come to take His children home, and we shall fall at His feet and sing, "Holy, Holy, Holy. Lord God Almighty!" The work on earth will be over and we shall praise Him through the ceaseless ages of eternity.

My Personal Application

In the final scenes of earth's history, God will use church administrators, pastors, and lay people in a final movement to reach the world with His end-time message. A revived church, unified in His love, will witness of His glory. Here is a prophecy of what is to come.

In visions of the night, representations passed before me of a great reformatory movement among God's people. Many were praising God. The sick were healed, and other miracles were wrought. A spirit of intercession was seen, even as was manifested before the great Day of Pentecost. Hundreds and thousands were seen visiting families and opening before them the word of God. Hearts were convicted by the power of the Holy Spirit, and a spirit of genuine conversion was manifest. On every side doors were thrown open to the proclamation of the truth. The world seemed to be lightened with the heavenly influence. Great blessings were received by the true and humble people of God. I heard voices of thanksgiving and praise, and there seemed to be a reformation such as we witnessed in 1844 (*Testimonies,* vol. 9, p. 126).

Did the Lord's messenger see you in that vision? Are you part of this last-day revival? Do you have a heartfelt burden for your family, friends, and neighbors? Here are some practical things you can do to share God's last-day message.

1. Ask God to impress you with somebody to share His love with.
2. As the Holy Spirit impresses you, share a piece of literature or book with this person.
3. At the appropriate time, invite them to study the Bible with you or join a small Bible study group.